P9-CJQ-077

MEMORY IMPROVEMENT

How To Improve Your Memory In Just 30 Days

Ron White

Published by:
Laurenzana Press
PO Box 1220
Melrose, FL 32666 USA

Copyright © 2010-2013 by Ron White

All rights reserved. No part of this book may be
reproduced in any form or by any means without the
prior written permission of the Publisher.

ISBN13: 978-1-937918-76-7

Get Your Bonus Video of
USA Memory Champion Ron White
teaching you:

- How to Give Speeches Without Notes

- How to Memorize Poems, Quotes and Scriptures

- How to Memorize Math and Chemistry Formulas

- How to Easily Memorize Six and Seven-Digit Numbers

- How to Memorize a Deck of Playing Cards

http://www.increase-your-memory.com

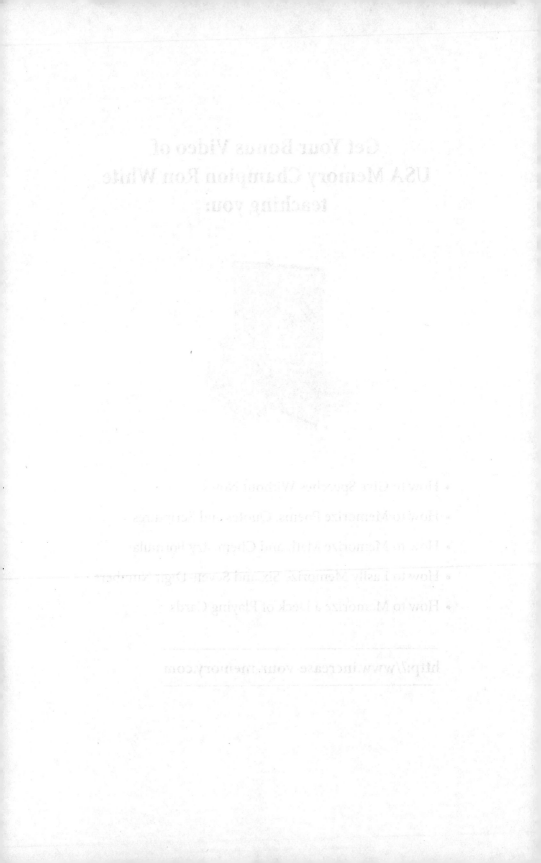

Table of Contents

Intro to Memory Training

Hello, and welcome to our "How to Improve Your Memory In Just 30 Days" program!

Psychologists tell us that if we do anything for 21 days or more it will become a habit. This program is carefully designed to help you make instant recall memory a habit. What you have in your hands is what I believe to be the most comprehensive program of its nature. Enjoy it.

This program is divided into 30 sections to be completed in thirty days, however you may progress at your own pace. It should take you about ten minutes a day. If you get excited and want to do more than one lesson in a day, there is certainly no harm in that!

We will start out with the very basics – so don't get bored during the simple stuff. Believe it or not, the simple basics are going to be the foundation for the advanced techniques. By the time you finish this program, you will have a PHD in memory training.

I want to begin this program by issuing you a challenge. Over the past few years I have made some observations of people after they have purchased a book, or invested in a workshop. The average investment for our live workshop is over $250 per person, and what is unbelievable to me is that one in five of the people who enroll never attend the class after making the investment. They invest over $250, and then never attend. As incredible as that may sound, I know that the average person who invests in a program of any nature – whether it is memory training, sales, public speaking, or something else, never completes the program. I know countless individuals whose libraries are filled with courses never completed. My challenge to you is this – Complete this course! When you do, you will have received some invaluable training.

Over the past several years I've used this training to give speeches or presentations that lasted several hours, and never accessed a single note. I've been in an elevator and recalled the name of a man I met for five minutes in a business environment a year and a half before. That simple act of recalling his name made him feel significant, and it turned into a great business contact for me. It is not exciting that I have done these things. What is exciting is that anyone who completes this course can do the same things.

Are you ready to begin? Are you excited? I know I am. It is important that you are willing to accept change.

The stages a person goes through when they encounter positive change are:

1. **Rejection.** We are creatures of habit, and anything new is often scoffed at.

2. **Unable to see their use for it.** You might say, "Well, Ronnie, I can see how this program has worked for you, and I can see how my kids and especially my spouse could use it, but it's not for me."

3. **Giving it a try.** As the walls of resistance begin to crumble you say, "I think I'll try it on a limited basis."

4. **Amazement.** "How did I ever get along without it?"

Do you remember going through these stages with the microwave oven? I do. At first you thought, "No way, why would I use that? What is the purpose? "The good old oven was good enough for my parents, and it's good enough for me." "If it doesn't say 'simmer,' then I'm not going to use it." At the next stage you will say, "Well, I can see how my kids might use it for a quick snack." Gradually you will come to say, "Maybe I can use it every now and then to warm up leftovers." Finally, "How did I get along without it?" What percentage of meals do you use a microwave for now? I bet a lot. We accept change slowly, that is the fourth level of positive change. Being cautious is not always a bad thing. It is good to be cautious and ease into new things, however, being too cautious and too slow is dangerous.

If you decide to fish, fine. If you decide to cut bait, fine. But if you do nothing, nobody eats. I ran into a woman at the Dallas/Fort Worth Airport who had attended my seminar. I said, "Colleen, how are you?" She jumped and she was so impressed that I remembered her name. I said, "Why are you impressed? You came to the workshop. You know what I'm doing. Sure it's been eight months since I met you along with a hundred other people, but you can do that too, Colleen, you know the system." She said, "Yes," she knows the system, and she thinks it's great, but she hasn't used it to the extent she should have.

Every single person who takes this course will fall into one of two categories.

1. They see value in the system and implement it into their daily lives – whether it is slowly, or all at once.

2. They see value in the system, but because of the change that is required, fall back on the old method of no memory system.

Right now, I want you to decide which category that you are going to be in. Give the system the benefit of the doubt right now, since you haven't actually learned the techniques. Tell yourself that you are not going to oppose this change, and you will see yourself recalling names, faces, numbers, and giving speeches without notes. In every aspect of life, not just memory training, there are comfort zones. It is hard to perform outside of the comfort zones. We get used to a way of doing things, and it is hard to change. A headline out of a local Seattle paper a few years ago, read, "*Justice Grinds Slow, Man Wants Back In Jail.*" According to the newspaper article, the man was released from a penitentiary, and found his eight weeks of freedom to be terrifying. Most of us would find eight weeks in a penitentiary terrifying. Why would eight weeks on the streets be terrifying to this man? It was terrifying because he was outside of his self-image comfort zone.

What happens when we are out of our comfort zone? Don't we have a tendency to get back where we belong, even though that is far short of what our potential could be? This man robbed a bank in Portland, Oregon and waited to be caught. He appeared before the judge without any legal counsel. He said, "Why do I need counsel, I'm a 10-time loser?" He said, "I would appreciate it if you forgo the pre-sentence investigation so that I can go back home tomorrow." "Home," in the article, he says, "I want to go <u>home</u>." Prison to him was home, it was a place he felt secure. It was his comfort zone.

What is the imaginary ceiling in your life? Folks – change is tough. Hopefully, no one reading this book will ever experience this situation, however I see people do this, to different degrees, every day. They are comfortable with the way they are doing things now, and the idea of change is scary, even if it is for the best for them. The change could be a diet; exercise; learning a foreign language; moving to a new town; going to a new school; or learning a method to recall information. Don't sell yourself short. Give yourself some credit. You have taken the action step to obtain this information, and now you are reading it. Don't stop here. Let me repeat that – DON'T STOP HERE!

What you are about to learn is over 2,500 years old. Can you believe these techniques have been around that long? In 477 BC, a Greek poet amazed everyone with his great memory. The story goes that the poet Simonides was at a banquet, and had just left the building when the roof caved in and killed many of those attending. The bodies had to be identified, but they were crushed beyond recognition. Simonides came to the rescue, and was able to recall the names of everyone, and where they sat. Simonides claimed he did this by imagining the people in their places at the table during the banquet. Subsequently, a method of recalling information was derived in part from this experience.

The Greeks developed a form of memory training called Loci, a Latin word meaning "places". We will go into more specific detail as to how this method works, and how it can work for you, shortly.

In 1959, there was another breakthrough in the area of memory. A brain surgeon, Wilder Penfield, conducted some remarkable experiments on epileptic patients. Penfield found that, when he touched parts of the patient's brain with a weak electronic stimulation, the fully conscious patient would begin talking, shouting and start to describe memories from years past – as if re-living the experience all over again. This demonstration proved that individual memories take up residence in different parts of the brain.

Similarly, different portions of the brain perform different functions. For example, the left side of your brain handles language skills. People who have suffered damage to a particular area of their brain might have trouble learning abstract concepts, but they are able to play the piano or hit a baseball as well as they ever did. The tissues of your brain shares communication with the rest of the body. The better you treat your body and your brain, through nutrition, avoiding substance abuse, and maintaining a good physical condition, the better it will work for you. Your brain is so wonderful and complex, that its origin cannot be an accident. It has been said that if your mind were simple enough to understand, you would be so simple that you couldn't understand it. So enjoy the 2,500-year-old techniques that you are about to learn, and remember – you are the greatest computer ever created.

* * *

Attention All Eagle Eyes: We've had a number of people proof this book before we released it to you, but there is a chance you might spot something that was missed. If you find a typo or other obvious error please send it to us. And if you're the first one to report it, we'll send you a free gift! Send to: corrections@laurenzanapress.com

Basic Association

Let's progress together to the next level of memory skills. I want to begin with some mental gymnastics to get your mind stimulated. Clear your mind of everything. Ok? Now, pick any number between 1 and 10. You got it? Now, multiply that number by 9. You should have a new number, now take the digits in this new number and add them together. For example, if your new number is 12, add 1 plus 2 and you get 3. Now, take that new number and subtract 5 from it. Got it? If not, back up and try again. Now assign that number a letter of the alphabet. For example, if the number you come up with after choosing a number between 1 and 10, multiplying by 9, adding the two digits together and subtracting 5 is 1, assign the letter A to this number; B if the number is 2; C if the number is 3; D if the number is 4; E if the number is 5; …and so on.

Next, think of a country that starts with the letter you just picked. Once you have the country, take the second letter in the name of that country and come up with the name of an animal that starts with that letter. Now choose a normal color for that animal. Are you thinking of a gray elephant from Denmark? Wow, huh! Can I read your mind, or what? Hardly, I just played a simple game with you. Regardless of the number chosen, 90% of you will end up with Denmark. It's a fun game that you can play with your friends.

I wanted to do that demonstration for two reasons:

1. I wanted to get your mind stimulated before we dive right in to the exercise.

2. I wanted to illustrate a point. What I just did was a game that you can play with your friends. That is the extent of the application of that brainteaser. What you are going to learn in this system is just as much fun as a game to do with your friends, however, please do not see that as the application for this system.

Recently, I ran into a guy while I was out to dinner who had taken our live training course. I said, "Hey, Ken, have you used the memory system? " He said, "Yeah, I won $100 off a friend of mine who didn't believe that I could memorize a list of 40 items after hearing it once – forwards, backwards, and by number. " We both laughed. I do hope, however, that Ken understands the application for this system is to recall product knowledge; give speeches without notes; remembering customer names; remembering to call important clients; recalling key points to a selling presentation; or helping students study. Practice by doing demonstrations with your friends, it is fun and good practice, but don't see this system as simply a game. If you do, you are cheating yourself, and I wouldn't bet your friends $100 either – or they probably won't be your friends much longer. Come to think of it, when I ran into Ken he was eating alone. So, let's have some fun, but also learn and remember that this system is going to help us in every aspect of our life.

When you decided to take action and invest in this training, you probably had just heard me on the radio, or doing a memory demonstration on TV or YouTube. Perhaps this training was given to you by a close friend or business associate who told you about a demonstration that I did, like having someone call off 15 or 20 items rapid fire, and I then repeated the list forwards and backwards. I'm going to do that same activity right now, only I am going to give YOU a list of 20 items and YOU are going to recall them. Use whatever memory system you normally use. This is just simply a test to give us a starting point, so sit back, relax, clear your mind of all thoughts, and remember – don't write this information down, this is a memory test. I'm going to give you 20 items to focus on. I want you to memorize this list in this EXACT order. The rules are: only go through this list ONCE, and spend no more than 5-7 seconds on each item. Have a sheet of paper ready to write down the items you remember (without looking at the list) afterwards.

1. Pencil
2. Sink
3. Circus
4. Track
5. Star
6. Bullet
7. Dice
8. Hourglass
9. Baseball
10. Fingers
11. Goalpost
12. Eggs
13. Flag
14. Necklace
15. Paycheck
16. Car
17. Magazine
18. Soldier
19. Golf Clubs
20. Shotgun

How many that you recall? Did you get all 20? Most people get anywhere between 3 and 5. If you got 6 or more, that is great! More than 10 items, is definitely above average.

Did you remember the items in the same order as listed? This is important as well. As an example of why: If I knew all 7 digits of a phone number, but did not remember in which order the numbers went, I'd be on the phone awhile.

Everything done in this program is done for a purpose. We will never complete an exercise that does not have at least one application. This exercise has three applications!

First, exactly as I stated before, it is simply a memory test to give us a starting point of reference. In other words, I wanted you to find out what your memory capabilities are before you begin to learn this system. So, write down how many you got correct and circle it. Did you notice anything different about this system that starts with a pencil? You may have noticed that some of the items related to the numbers. For example, number 16 was a car and you get a driver's license when you are 16. Number 3 was a circus, and we have all heard of a 3-ring circus. Every item on this list could actually have been associated with a number in some way. Now, I know what you're thinking. Ron, you said this system was not basic association. It's not. You do, however, need to have an understanding of what basic association is before we can elevate you to higher forms of memory training.

We are going to begin with association – which is first grade in terms of memory training. This is called the "pencil list" because it starts with a pencil. It is a basic association list. Let me show you what I mean. Picture an image associated to each number.

- Number one is a pencil. The association is that the numeral one looks like a pencil.

- Number 2 is a sink. The association for 2 and sink is that it has 2 knobs, and 2 options – on and off, hot and cold. Someone in a workshop once said that if you look at the pipes under a sink, the way they twist and bend kind of looks like a number 2. Now that's an imagination, but that is exactly what it takes to recall.

- Number 3 is a circus. The association is a 3-ring circus.

- Number 4, the association here is that are 4 lanes in a track; 4 times around is a mile. Remember the 4-minute mile?

- Number 5 is a star. What would the star and the number 5 have in common? If you said a star has five points, that's a good association. A star has 5 points.

- Number 6 is a bullet. What about this one? If a bullet shoots you, you're 6 feet under, right? There are 6 bullets in a chamber – a six-shooter.

- Number 7 is dice. Seven come 11, lucky 7. Do you know that opposite sides of dice always add up to 7? Now, what was number 5? Star, right, because it has 5 points. What about 2, sink, 2 knobs. How about 7, dice, right? Seven come 11, opposite sides always equal 7. If there is a 2 on the top, the 5 will be on the bottom. What about number 4, track, right? Four lanes, 4-minute mile, 4 laps is one mile. Remember, this is what is called basic association. It is very basic, and all it requires is that you visualize and associate.

- Number 8 is an hourglass, an 8 looks like an hourglass because of its shape.

- Number 9 is a baseball. In baseball there are 9 innings, and 9 players on a team. Last year the Rangers blew a 9-run lead in the ninth. Now, what was two? Think about it. Sink, right? Number 3, circus, right? How about 7? Dice. Seven come 11.

- Number 10 is fingers. I would be willing to say that most of you have 10 fingers and 10 toes, so 10 is fingers.

- Number 11 is a goal post. There are 11 players on each football team. When a field goal is kicked, the referee makes his arms go up like an 11. What about 5? Star, right? Five points on a star. What was 9? Baseball, right? Nine innings, 9 players. How about 6? It was bullet. Six feet under.

- Number 12 is eggs. A dozen eggs, that one is pretty easy.

- Number 13 is a flag. What do you think the associations for 13 and flag are? Do you think of the original 13 colonies? Did you know that there are 13 stripes on our current flag? What was 10? Finger, right? Ten fingers and toes. Hold out your hands and say 10. If someone gives you 5 on both hands, that's 10! If you have a 10-dollar bill, you wrap your fingers around it so you don't lose it.

- Number 14 is a necklace. Fourteen karat gold; Valentine's Day is February 14th. A necklace could be a Valentine's Day gift.

- Number 15 is a paycheck. When do a lot of people get paid? The first and the 15th, right? Now, what if you don't get paid on the 15th? What if I told you that on the 15th of every month, I had a check for $15,000 waiting for you in my office? Would you ever forget to come by my office on the 15th? So, 15 is what? A paycheck, right?

- Number 16 is a car. When do you get a driver's license? Sixteen, right?

- Number 17 is a magazine. Some of you men may not know that there is a magazine for teenage girls called *Seventeen*. So what was 17? Magazine, right? Remember, it is a magazine. How about number 14? Remember, it was necklace, 14 karat gold, Valentine's Day.

- Number 18 is a soldier. When is someone eligible for the draft? Eighteen, right?

- Nineteen is golf clubs. How many holes are on a golf course? No, not 19, there are eighteen. You golfers know that the 19th hole is where you go after the eighteenth hole to relax and have something to eat or drink.

- Number 20. Twenty is a shotgun. Twenty and shotgun. Ever heard of a 20-gauge shotgun?

Remember that this list was created using the first generation, the first level of memory training called association. It works, but very seldom. In other words, we associated 9 with baseball – 9 innings and 9 players. If number 3 was a baseball, that wouldn't work, would it? We couldn't use basic association because 3 and baseball have nothing in common. However, basic association does play a significant role in memory training, and it is important to understand. What was number two? Think about it. Two knobs, the pipes look like a 2, hot and cold. Two is a sink, right?

Now I want you to get a very vivid picture in your mind of a sink. Perhaps, it could be the sink in your kitchen or bathroom, the location is not important. What is important is to get a clear picture in your mind. Your mind thinks in pictures. For example, clear your mind of every thought. I want you to now think of anything <u>but</u> a dog. Don't see a dog. What happened? You thought of a dog, didn't you? What that illustrates is your mind thinks in pictures. You don't see the word, dog spelled out, you actually see a dog. Your eye is the strongest part of the memory. That is why when you see a person, you say, I recognize the face, but what is their name? That is because you saw their face. You never saw their name.

Since we know that we recall what we see longer than what we simply hear, remember to actually visualize these items – and the bigger, the better. Make the pictures larger than life. What was 7? Seven come 11. It was dice, so imagine a huge, furry, man-eating dice. The dice are so big that you can't even see over them. Remember, visualize a huge dice. Next, what was 12? ….Eggs. A dozen eggs. Visualize 12 eggs. Maybe they are on the floor, and you're breaking them. Next, what was 5?..... It has 5 points – a star. Good. Get a clear picture of a star with 5 points. What was 10?..... Fingers. Ten fingers, 10 toes, holding onto a 10-dollar bill. What was 14?..... Fourteen karat gold, Valentine's Day. Get a good picture of necklace in your mind. What was 17?..... Magazine. What was 8? Hourglass. What was 11?.... Goal posts. How about track?..... That was 4. Four lanes, 4 laps. Do you remember 13? Thirteen stars, 13 stripes?

What about 15?..... Paycheck. The first and the 15th? I know that you won't forget that one.

What was number one? ...Pencil. A pencil is a straight line like a number one. Remember that this is called the pencil list because it starts with pencil.

What about number 18? Soldier. Eighteen to join the military.

What about 20?... Shotgun. Twenty-gauge shotgun.

What about 19?... That's golf clubs. Remember the 19th hole?

What about 16?... That's car. At 16, you get your driver's license.

What was number two? ... It was sink.

Number 4, track; number 6, bullet; number 9, baseball; number thirteen, flag; number seventeen, magazine; number eighteen, soldier. Remember, that this is what is called basic association. It does have its applications, however, if you try to use it for everything you're going to be up the creek in a wire boat without a paddle.

It is time to stop, and let's write down this list one more time. If you get stuck on one, skip it and go to the next one, it might come to you. Ask yourself, what was the association? Don't spend more than 4 or 5 minutes on this exercise.

Ok, how did you do? Probably a lot better than the first time for sure. Let's see, just follow along and put a check mark on the ones you got correct. Remember, they do have to be in the correct order and by the correct number.

1. Pencil

2. Sink

3. Circus

4. Track

5. Star

6. Bullet

7. Dice

8. Hourglass

9. Baseball

10. Fingers

11. Goal Post

12. Eggs

13. Flag

14. Necklace

15. Paycheck

16. Car

17. Magazine

18. Soldier

19. Golf Clubs

20. Shotgun

Did you get a better score this time? I bet you did! What we just did was an exercise in basic association. Did you get all 20? If you did, that's great! Most everyone should get at least 15 or more. If you got less than 15, the reason is that when you created the associations, the pictures were not vivid enough. Remember that your mind thinks in pictures, and remembers pictures, not words or abstract thoughts. So, make an effort to actually visualize everything you are attempting to recall using this system. Make your pictures huge and larger than life – the bigger the better. Don't see number 7 as small dice in a Monopoly game, visualize 7-foot tall man-eating dice. I promise you that if you saw that, you would never forget it. So, see it.

You have just completed our first lesson. I know it was basic; however, you must crawl before you walk. This course will slowly elevate you through the levels of memory techniques, until eventually you will have a Masters Degree in memory training. This is what is called basic association. When I meet people, and I tell them that I teach memory training, they say, "Oh, association, I know all about that." Perhaps they do. However, memory training goes much deeper than that. Association is the first level. You have just completed Day 2. I know right now you're thinking that this is too basic, and you're right, we're at a very basic stage. Association can't be used for everything. However, you must understand it before we progress to the next level. Trust me – we are starting at the first grade level. Remember when you learned how to read, you had to learn the alphabet first. Then when you got to high school, you read Shakespeare. Day 2 is learning the alphabet. By the time we get to Day 30, you are going to have a PHD in memory training.

Chain of Visualization

The next level of association includes elements of memory training, such as acronyms. Have you heard of acronyms? An acronym is a series of letters using the first letter of each word. IBM is an acronym for International Business Machines. AT&T is an acronym for American Telephone and Telegraph. Companies use these because they are easier to remember. When I was in high school, my science teacher told me that I could learn the colors of the rainbow in the correct order by remembering the name Roy G Biv.

R for red, O for orange, y for yellow, G for green, B for blue, I for indigo, and V for violet. Another acronym I learned in school was an easy way to remember the Great Lakes – H.O.M.E.S. H for Huron; O for Ontario; M for Michigan; E for Erie; and S for Superior. That is an easy way to learn the Great Lakes.

Can acronyms be used for everything? No. Are there more advanced ways to retain information? Yes, however, every level of memory training is important, and you never know when a good old-fashioned acronym is what you need to use to recall some vital information. Remember, this course is meant to be learned in levels. I'm sure that right now, at this point, you would love to know how to memorize a 100-digit number after only hearing it once. Believe me, we will get there. Patience is the key. You can't skip any steps. Believe it or not, we are going to use the pencil list later to learn how to count in Japanese. I know you find that hard to believe right now, but just watch. You're going to be amazed.

Have you ever heard about how a bamboo tree grows? You'll water it every day for five years and see nothing. And one day, in the fifth year, it will grow several feet in a period of a few weeks. Did it grow in a few weeks or 5 years? It obviously grew in five years. But, the results were seen in the few weeks because of the work put in before then. Your memory is the same way. Right now, we are watering it, but by the end of this program it is going to grow very large, very quickly.

Acronyms and links are in this "watering" stage. A link is a method of recalling information by telling a story. Many ancient books, such as the Bible, were passed down from one generation to the next this way. I bet you can sing many of your favorite tunes on the radio and not miss a beat. The reason is that you have, number one, incorporated the link method of memorizing by connecting one thought to the next. Songs also incorporate rhythm, which helps your memory. A link is simply connecting one thought to the next. For example, here is a list of 19 items. If I ask you to memorize them using basic association, it would not work. For example, number one is Mount Rainier; number 2 is ice; number 3 is trees; number 4 is bicycle. What do these items have in common with the number they are with? Nothing that I am aware of. So, in this case, basic association would not work.

The next level is the chain of association or the link. Sit back, relax and enjoy this story. I want you to focus on seeing the images in this story very clearly, vividly and powerfully. Here is the story:

Mount Rainier has ice on the top, and trees on the side. Coming down the mountain is a bicycle, ridden by a German shepherd. He has a glass of water in one hand, and a shoe in the other. At the bottom of the mountain he crashes into a TV set and lands on a pillow. He bounces off the pillow onto a trampoline, and bounces off the trampoline into an airplane. The airplane lands in Dallas, and Richard Nixon is waiting for him. Nixon has on a brown hat and black boots. He hands him a check for $50,000 and the keys to a brand new Corvette. He then drives the Corvette back to Mount Rainier.

Now, we're going to do this one more time. The difference is I want you to repeat the items out loud. By the way, if you move your hands and use body language, you'll have reinforced the pictures in your mind. So, here we go. Sit back and read this story again.

Mount Rainier has ice on the top, and trees on the side. Repeat with me. Mount Rainier has ice on the top, and trees on the side. Coming down the mountain is a bicycle, ridden by a German Shepherd. Repeat with me. Coming down the mountain is a bicycle, ridden by a German Shepherd. He has a glass of water in one hand, and a shoe in the other. Repeat with me. He has a glass of water in one hand, and a shoe in the other. At the bottom of the mountain he crashes into a TV set. Repeat with me. At the bottom of the mountain he crashes into a TV set. He lands on a pillow, bounces on a trampoline, and bounces off the trampoline into an airplane. Repeat with me. He lands on a pillow, bounces on a trampoline, and bounces off the trampoline into an airplane. The airplane lands in Dallas, and Richard Nixon is waiting for him. Repeat with me. The airplane lands in Dallas, and Richard Nixon is waiting for him. Nixon has on a brown hat and black boots. Repeat with me. Nixon has a brown hat and black boots. He hands him a check for $50,000 and the keys to a brand new Corvette. Repeat with me. He hands him a check for $50,000 and the keys to a brand new Corvette. He then drives the Corvette back to Mount Rainier. Repeat with me. He then drives the Corvette back to Mount Rainier.

Did you use body language with it? I always do. I hold out my hands like I'm holding a glass of water and a shoe. I bounce like I'm on the trampoline and I act like I'm Richard Nixon, and I stick out my hands like they have keys and $50,000 in them.

Let's do this one more time. Here we go. Focus on the story:

Mount Rainier has ice on the top, and trees on the side. Repeat with me. Mount Rainier has ice on the top, and trees on the side. Coming down the mountain is a bicycle, ridden by a German Shepherd. Repeat with me. Coming down the mountain is a bicycle, ridden by a German Shepherd. He has a glass of water in one hand, and a shoe in the other. Repeat with me. He has a glass of water in one hand, and a shoe in the other. At the bottom of the mountain he crashes into a TV set. Repeat with me. At the bottom of the mountain he crashes into a TV set. He lands on a pillow, bounces on a trampoline, and bounces off the trampoline into an airplane. Repeat with me. He lands on a pillow, bounces on a trampoline, and then bounces off the trampoline into an airplane. The airplane lands in Dallas, and Richard Nixon is waiting for him. Repeat with me. The airplane lands in Dallas, and Richard Nixon is waiting for him. Nixon has on a brown hat and black boots. Repeat with me. Nixon has a brown hat and black boots. He hands him a check for $50,000, and the keys to a brand new Corvette. Repeat with me. He hands him a check for $50,000, and the keys to a brand new Corvette. He then drives the Corvette back to Mount Rainier. Repeat with me. He then drives the Corvette back to Mount Rainier.

Now it is time to see how many that you recalled. On a sheet of paper, write down all the items in this list. Don't write out the story, instead, simply write each noun in the story. For example, Mount Rainer will be the first item on the list.

Set the book aside now and write down the items there are 16 items. Do not spend more than 4-5 minutes on this exercise. After you done come back and check your answers. Answers below:

1. Mount Rainier

2. Bicycle

3. German Shepherd

4. Glass of water

5. Shoe

6. TV set

7. Pillow

8. Trampoline

9. Airplane

10. Dallas

11. Richard Nixon

12. Brown hat

13. Black boots

14. Check for $50,000

15. Keys to a brand new Corvette

16. Mount Rainier

How did you do? Did the link method work for you? I bet you did pretty well. Our minds are truly the greatest computers ever created, and I mean that. Don't get caught up in being perfect right now. Just make sure that you understand the concepts before we progress to the next level. Remember that this course is a building block process. Make sure you understand basic association, acronyms, and the link method before you move on.

Day 4

A 2000 Year Old Memory Method

Radio certainly has entertained millions over the years, and the great radio programs of the 30's, 40's and 50's are now classics. What an experience that must have been, sitting by the radio creating your own pictures of the stories that were being told. I bet everyone listening had different images of the characters – what they looked like, what they wore, what their families looked like. That is the beauty of the imagination, and the power of the mind. I am a huge Texas Rangers baseball fan. I can remember listening to the Ranger games on the radio late at night, when I was 12 and 13. I can remember the pictures I created in my head. I remember visualizing the baseball, and the sounds of the crowd that evoked the pictures and emotions that I felt when I was actually there.

Imagine this – A huge lemon is sitting on the table in front of you. Can you see it? It is the size of a grapefruit. Take your right hand and visualize yourself cutting down the middle of that lemon. See the juices oozing all over the tablecloth. Sitting on the table are two halves of the lemon. Pick up one piece of the lemon and hold that half up to your nose. Do you smell the lemon? Is the moisture from the lemon getting your nose wet? Now, with the hand holding the lemon against your mouth, open your mouth as wide as you can, and think of the meat of that lemon in your mouth. Bite down on the lemon and let the juices drip down your face.

Did you salivate? Did your face squish up into a bitter expression? The next question you should be asking yourself is why did I make those expressions? What provoked them? Your mind thinks in pictures, and often it cannot tell the difference between an actual picture, and a picture that exists in your mind only. Your mind truly is incredible. That is why athletes visualize their successes – their golf swings, batting swings, or catching footballs – long before they actually do those things because their minds believe that it is real. If the visualization is strong enough, then you are actually conditioning your mind for success with pictures. Your mind utilizes pictures to retain information, and we are going to use that knowledge to our benefit. Pay close attention to next few thoughts; they are going to be the nuts and bolts of this program. Everything will build on them, so this is very important. What we are about to learn is actually the system that the Romans developed 2,500 years ago.

Remember the Loci we talked about (Latin word for places)? The Romans actually developed places in their minds where they would store information. They discovered that your mind actually works like a filing system. Here's a modern day example. Most of us use computers in some fashion. It is hard to get by without one. When you have information you wish to keep, what do you do? You store it on a disk, a CD, print it and file it. Let me create a picture that might be a horror story for some of you who work with computers.

Let's say a hacker got into your computer and deleted all of your directories, files and program titles. Everything was still in your computer hard drive, but it was no longer labeled. Wouldn't that be a mess? The information would still be in there, but finding it would be a big problem. The analogy is this: everything you have ever seen, heard, or done is still in your memory. Accessing and retrieving it is the difficult part. Many students have told me that when they are taking a test, they know the information but they don't remember it until the test is over a few hours later. They knew it; they just couldn't get the information out of their memories when they needed it. This will happen with business professionals when they leave out a part of their presentation, and then recall it when the meeting is over. The stress is gone and your mind is freed up to bring it back. Unfortunately, it is obviously too late then. So, just like the computer, the information is in there, it's finding it when you need it that is the problem. The system the Romans developed allows you to create files and directories in your mind, and store information in those files. Sounds pretty cool, doesn't it? Well, guess what? It is…..it's very cool. It has transformed my life.

Remember, I told you to listen closely, because the next part will be the nuts and bolts of memory training. Well, here it is. The Romans discovered that you need five things to recall anything – numbers, poems, scripture, dates, presentations or names. The items are the same your computer uses.

1. Focus

2. Location

3. Code

4. Action

5. Review

The first item of business is <u>focus</u>. You must consciously focus your memory. There are many supplements that you can take to focus your memory, and one of my favorites is the Omega-3 Fish Oil capsule. Adding this supplement to your diet does a number of benefits to your health, including increasing your memory and ability to focus. You will be able to find this naturally in some foods, like pink ocean fish, spinach and blueberries.

Foods good for memory:

Spinach

Blueberries

Red Onions

Apples

Red Beets

Grapes

Cherries

Eggplant

Rosemary

Next, when you store information on your computer, where do you put it? You put it in a <u>file or directory</u> to retrieve it later. Your mind works the same way. The <u>code</u> your memory recognizes is pictures, so we turn everything we want to recall into a picture. This is the code our mind thinks in. Number 4 on our list is <u>action</u>. What holds the code in the file on the computer? The circuits hold the information in a storage unit until it is deleted. Action is the circuit for our memories. That may not make sense right now, but it will as we progress. So you may be saying to yourself, "Great, Ron, but where is the place I can mentally store information?" I don't have circuits in my head. Believe it or not, you do.

As Wilder Penfield discovered in 1959, you actually have files in your mind right now, and you don't even know it. Can you believe that? It's true. Here are some landmarks about the town that you live in. Can you visualize the school? What about the fire department, your home, the police station, maybe a public swimming pool, a river, the park, a hotel, a car dealership or a restaurant. Could you visualize those things? I bet you could. They are there. They exist. These are what the Romans called files. What the Romans would do is start at the north end of their town, and then chooses an item – like a park; a river; a stadium; a tree; or an object that stands out, and that would be their first file. As they moved south through the town, they would choose items in a very systematic north to south method, until they had maybe 25 or 30 files. Some probably had many more files. Your town could actually be a file system.

I had the good fortune to live in downtown Seattle in my twenties and I took a job as a waiter. On one of my first days there I was asked to learn the food menu. Did I use this opportunity to spotlight my memory? Sure I did. A little showing off is good every now and then. What I did was pick buildings around Seattle as my files. The space needle was my number one file. The King Dome was number 2. Safeco Field was number 3, and other restaurants and buildings were my files until I had about 20. I even used the bay and some of the piers. Remember, the next step in recalling information is to turn it into a code that your mind remembers, and that code is what? The code our minds use to remember with is – pictures, so, I turned the menu items into pictures and filed them using action. What is action, you ask? Good question, but wait just a minute before we get to that part.

Remember, you are a bamboo tree. I impressed everyone with how easy I was able to do this using my newly created city files. I started conversations, and I even taught people I worked with how to do it. It even helped me make friends. You didn't know this course could do that, did you? Pretty cool, huh? So right now you should be getting a general idea how this system works, but not exactly. Right now you may be thinking, "This sounds fascinating!" But perhaps you don't see exactly how it works until you see the application. If that is how you are thinking, then good. That's exactly where you should be. If you were supposed to understand everything right now, we would stop the program here. We aren't going to do that.

In a moment you are going to draw out your own 'City Files'. What you need to do is visualize your town from a bird's eye view. The top of the page is the North, and pick 10 items that you can use as files. Remember, good files are buildings, restaurants, schools, houses or even a gas station. Remember to do this in a systematic way. Work north to south, east to west, or even clockwise – just make it logical. As you draw a box or diagram to denote the file, place a number beside it, one through 10.

Here is an example of what your city files might look like:

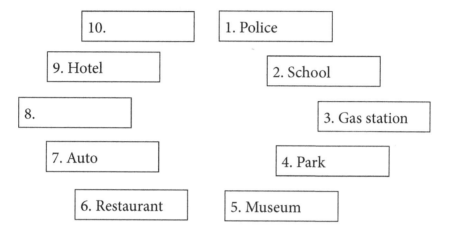

Once again, pick 10 files in your city, write them down, and then memorize them!

How did you do? Did you zip right through it? You have just created your first 10 files. It should be kind of exciting. Now, let's not beat around the bush any longer, let's use them. I'm going to give you 10 pictures, and we are going to file them to your 10 city files. Again, what are the 5 things you need to recall anything?

1. Focus

2. Location

3. Code

4. Action

5. Review

Before we dive right in, let me ask you a few questions. Can you remember every time you've gotten in a car and driven somewhere? Most of us can't. But I bet you can tell me the time you were driving and someone pulled out in front of you and your cars collided. You could probably tell me the time of day, where you were going, what you were driving, who was with you, and what they were wearing. Now, the question is, why? What is the difference? That picture was vivid and it had emotions tied to it. I bet you can't tell me every time you have gone to see a movie, or had dinner with someone. I bet you remember that first date, or your first break up? Those are things that have emotion tied to them, and are stronger in our memories. So, the number 4 in our system is the action, and that is what we use to create the vivid picture with the emotion tied to it. The more vivid and emotional the action is, the better you will recall it. Just like the lemon analogy. It has to be vivid.

By now your city files need to be driven into your memory, and you need to know them forwards and backwards. Below you will find a list of 10 words. Using the city files that you have created, place each of these objects mentally on your location, and visualize it with action. If the first word you want to memorize is water, then see a giant glass of water pouring out onto your location. Remember the more vivid and larger than life your image, the better chance that you will recall it.

Here is the list. Scan through it as quickly as possible, and use the locations in your city files – imagine larger than life images, and here we go:

1. Photo Album

2. Igloo

3. Cactus

4. Noah's Ark

5. Gold bars

6. The color red

7. Doctor stitching a cut

8. Clothes made of dollar bills

9. Oranges

10. Peaches

Now write down the 10 pictures to test your recall. Don't write the file or the action down, just the picture. For example, number one, just write photo album. If you get stuck on one, don't worry about it. Don't get bogged down on one item. You can always come back to it later. Ask yourself, what was your file, and then the picture should come to you. When you complete this test, come back to the program.

So, how did you do? Did you get all 10 of them? If you did, pat yourself on the back – that is a great accomplishment. Remember, when you heard about this memory system, and you heard that I was able to hear items once and then recall them forwards, backwards, or by number – you were impressed. You were not impressed with the process; you were impressed with the results.

Once, a lady who attended one of our live classes in Dallas was disappointed because our system was so simple. I explained to her that is not a drawback – that is the beauty of this system. I have read every study and program done on memory training. I could make this course difficult and cumbersome, but why would I want to do that when you can get phenomenal results with such a simple process?

First 10 States in Alphabetical Order:

1. Alabama

2. Alaska

3. Arizona

4. Arkansas

5. California

6. Colorado

7. Connecticut

8. Delaware

9. Florida

10. Georgia

Now, how many did you get right? If you got 9 or 10, pat yourself on the back. If you got 8 or less, ask yourself why. It can only be one of two reasons. Either, number one, you did not know your file, or number two, your picture wasn't vivid enough. If you knew your file, but you missed it, it's because the picture wasn't strong enough. Make sure that you know your files by heart, and that the pictures that you create are vivid. By the way, did you know that I just taught you a list that actually means something, and you didn't even know it? Oftentimes, to recall something, we are going to have to turn an abstract into a picture. That is exactly what we just did. We turned 10 abstract words into pictures, and filed them to our files. Would you believe me if I just told you that you just learned the first 10 states of the United States in alphabetical order? Well, guess what? You did.

Remember, each state is an abstract word. We used a picture or something we could represent to see it. Let's see what I mean. What was number one? …. Photo album. The first state in alphabetical order is Alabama. A photo album for Alabama. Number two is igloo. What do you think that represents? Alaska, right? Number 3, cactus. Did you guess Arizona? If you did you're right. Number 4, Noah's Ark. Almost too easy. Arkansas. Number 5, gold bars. Where was the gold rush in 1849? California, of course. Number 6, the color red. How about Colorado? Number 7, stitching a cut? What are you doing? You are connecting a cut…. Connecticut. Connecting-a-cut. Number 8, dollar bill wear. Delaware. Dollar bill wear, Delaware. Number 9, oranges. What state is known for oranges? Florida, of course. Number 10, peaches. How about Georgia? There you have it! The first 10 states in alphabetical order. Did you think it was going to be that easy? You have learned quite a bit today. Stop and pick up tomorrow, on Day 5.

Skeleton Files

Are you ready to dig in and expand your memory? Let's review what we have learned on Day 4. To recall something, you must have 5 things – focus, a location, a code, an action and review. A location or a file is simply a place to store information; it could be anything at all. For example, the first building in your city files is your number one file. All 10 of the files work together in this filing system. Anything can be a filing system as long as it goes in a logical order, and you can see or visualize each item. For example, your car could be a filing system with 10 files. These could be your car files. Number one is your front bumper; number two is your hood or engine; number 3 is your front windshield; number 4 is your steering wheel; number 5 is your gear shift; number 6 could be your glove box; number 7 could be your passenger seat; number 8 could be the back seat; number 9 could be the trunk; and number 10 is your license plate. Remember, you don't have to use these as one of your filing systems, but you certainly can.

The reason I wanted to bring them up is to illustrate that anything can be a file system. Your favorite golf course could be an 18-file system. One of those holes may have a sand trap or water hazard next to it. That would be your file for that hole.

The Ballpark in Arlington, where the Texas Rangers play, is a file system for me. Number one is the pitcher's mound; number two is home plate; number 3 is first base; number 4 is second; and so on. Ok, do you get the idea now? We are going to create a file system that I think you're going to like. Its kind of fun.

There are 10 files in this system, and it is called our skeleton files. Why? Because the files are you! You are a file system. I bet you can visualize this. It is important to verbalize and touch your files. These are going to be permanent files for you, and you must call them what I call them – the reason will make sense later. This may be the most important file system you have learned up to this point, so are you ready for your next 10 files? Here we go! Number one is the top of your head. We are going to call it top. So, say top and touch the top of your head. I know that you may feel silly. You may say, "Ron, this is silly." Do you think so? Well, I will tell you what is silly, forgetting to call a client because you fail to remember, or giving a speech and forgetting what you are supposed to say. That, my friends, is silly.

This system is a little different, but have fun with it. So again, what was number one? It was the top of your head. So, say top and pat the top of your head. Your number two file is going to be your nose, so pat your nose and say number two. What was your one? One was top. What was number two? Two is nose. Your number 3 file is your mouth. Say mouth and then touch your mouth. What was one? Top. Two was nose, and 3 is mouth. Notice we're just moving from top to bottom. Your number 4 file is your ribs. So, grab your ribs and hold onto them and say number 4 is my ribs. What is number 4? It is your ribs. Your fifth file is your liver. It is right in the lower half of your torso. We are halfway through.

Number 6 is going to be your hip joint. We are going to call it joint. So, touch your number 6 file and say number 6 is my joint. What is 4? Ribs, right? What about number one? Top. What about 4? Ribs. What was number 6? Joint. Ok, our number 7 file is going to be your knee cap. We are just going to call it cap. So, 7 is cap. What is 7? Cap. Pat it and say number 7 is cap. What about 5? How about liver? What was 3? Mouth. What about number one? It was top.

Our number 8 file is going to be a bone in our lower leg. There are two bones in your lower leg, between your kneecap and ankle. One of them is your fibula, so repeat after me – number 8 is fibula. Touch your leg and repeat – number 8 is fibula. Number 9 is on the very bottom. It is the ball of your foot. We are going to call it ball. So, what is number 9? It is ball. Number 7 is cap; number 5, liver; number 4, ribs; number 6, joint. And number 10 is not on your skeleton. It is actually the ground. We are going to call it the sand. Point to the ground or the floor and say, number 10 is the sand.

Let's review quickly. Number one is top; two is nose; 3 is mouth; 4 is ribs; 5 is liver; 6 is joint; 7 is cap; 8 is fibula; 9 is ball; and 10 is sand. These are your 10 skeleton files, and it is very important that you know them. Stop and repeat each file. Here is a diagram now memorize it!

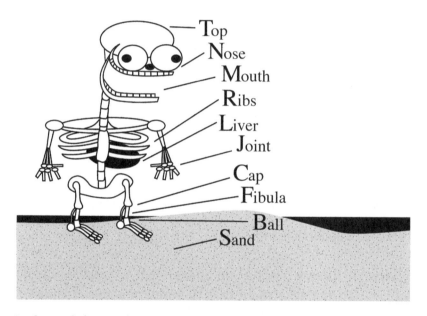

So how did you do? Pretty simple, right? You betcha! That is the beauty of this system. Later, believe it or not, the skeleton files are going to be instrumental in learning how to recall long digit numbers or phone numbers. Next, we are going to go through the same process as we did the city files. I am going to give you a list of words, and you are going to memorize them using your body as the storage location. If you need to stop and make sure that you know your skeleton files, then do that before proceeding. Are you ready? Clear your mind of all distractions.

Here is a list of 10 items. File the first one to your first skeleton file; and the second one to your second file; and so on. Move as fast as you can through this list. Don't wait until you are 100% certain that you have the image mentally glued. Force yourself to go faster than you think is doable and you will be amazed with your recall. However, keep it in perspective, the speed is not the crucial ingredient at this stage… understanding the system is the focus.

1. Speaker

2. Gun

3. Soldier

4. Spotlight

5. A picture of you

6. Judge riding a fast motorcycle

7. Jury

8. Excessive amount of money

9. Making a right turn with your hand over your mouth

10. State Capitol building

Review all 10 very quickly and attach them to your files as rapidly as you can. Do not take more than 1 minute on this, at most. Now, write down the 10 pictures we just filed. Rejoin the program when you complete this process.

Bill of Rights

1. Freedom of Speech

2. Right to Bear Arms

3. Protection From Quartering Troops

4. Freedom from Unreasonable Search and Seizure

5. Right to not Self-Incriminate

6. Right to Speedy Trial

7. Right to Trial by Jury

8. Prohibition of Excessive Bail

9. Protection of Rights Not Enumerated

10. Protection of State's Rights

How did you do? Did you get all 10? If not, ask yourself why – it is only for one of two reasons: either you didn't know your file; or your picture wasn't vivid enough. There are no other options. Remember, in order to recall something, you must turn an abstract into a picture. We just filed the first 10 Amendments to the Constitution – the Bill of Rights, to our skeleton files. Did you believe that we could do that? Well, we did. Many students spend all day saying the Bill of Rights over and over. You just learned it forwards, backwards, and by number in less than 5 minutes. You don't believe me? Let's see.

Number one was speaker. Well, speaker stands for freedom of speech. Number two, what did we file to the nose? A gun, right? That amendment says we have the right to bear arms. Number 3. What was 3? A Soldier. No soldier shall be quartered in a house without the consent of the owner. Number 4 was a spotlight. You had a spotlight on your ribs. Freedom from unreasonable search and seizure. For number 5 you had a picture of yourself in your liver, didn't you? No one will be called to testify against himself or herself. Number 6 was a judge riding a fast motorcycle. Remember, right there on your joint, you had a judge riding a fast motorcycle? That was an abstract to a speedy trial. Number 7, what was it? A jury of 12. That picture is representative of the right to a trial by jury. Number 8 is an excessive amount of money – remember? We had an excessive amount of money coming out of our fibula? That amendment states that there shall be no excessive bail. Number 9, what did we file to the ball of our foot? We filed you making a right hand turn with your hand over your mouth. This amendment says that people may have rights even if they are not mentioned in the constitution (hand over mouth for not mentioned), and these rights can still be violated. Number 10 is a state capitol, right? We had a state capitol on the sand? That amendment talked about state's rights.

Now, I think that you will agree that these pictures were somewhat unusual. When you are doing this on your own, you're going to have the freedom to make your own pictures. If you are a student, this example of application should be very obvious to you. If you're a business professional, I hope you can also see the application. The skeleton file could be used to recall a "things to do list," steps in a presentation; procedures; organization; mission statements; or to give a speech. The applications are endless. Each day, I am going to use generic examples, but please be creative. This system can truly change the way you go about your daily life if you let it. I encourage you to do that.

1. Focus

2. Location

3. Code

4. Action

5. Review

Pencil List Practice

Welcome back. It's now Day 6. Can you feel your memory expanding? I hope that this process is exciting for you. The system you are learning is just that. This is a very specific system in which business professionals and students from around the country, and for that matter – the world, are using to impact their lives. Now let's review. What are the 5 things you need to memorize anything? Number one, focus; next is a location or a file; number three is a code, which is the picture and number; four is action; and five is review. Remember, a file can be anything. It is simply a place in your mind that you can see or visualize. A file is a building in your city, or your nose, your mouth, or even a hole on your favorite golf course. It is also important to recall that each filing system has more than one file. For example, for your skeleton files you have top, nose, mouth, and so on. Each one of them is a file, however, when placed together they are a file system. As long as there is more than one of them, they should go in a logical order, you can see them, and they can be used as a file system. The only limit is your imagination. The code, as you recall, is the picture.

Computers translate everything they store to a code so they can recall it later. The computer between your ears works exactly the same way, and the code that your mind recalls is pictures. Your mind remembers pictures that are unusual and have emotion tied to them. If you are missing some items when we go back and review our list, it is for one of two reasons: Either you did not know your file, or you knew your file but did not know your information because the picture you created was not vivid enough. The circuit board in your memory is the glue that you create.

You have 10 skeleton files, and 10 city files. We learned the pencil list, and we learned how to use acronyms and the link method. These are all valid forms of memory training. We are going to cover giving speeches without notes; learning poems or scripture; product knowledge; things to do list; math formulas; foreign languages; and much more. Let's review our pencil list:

1. Pencil — 11. Goal Post

2. Sink — 12. Eggs

3. Circus — 13. Flag

4. Track — 14. Ring

5. Star — 15. Paycheck

6. Bullet — 16. Car

7. Dice — 17. Magazine

8. Hour Glass — 18. Soldier

9. Baseball — 19. Golf Clubs

10. Fingers — 20. Shotgun

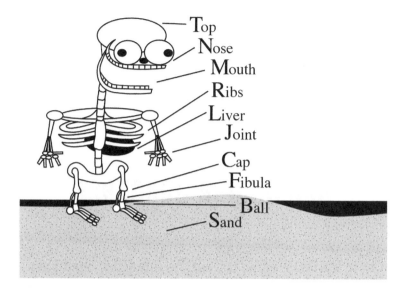

These are files, places where we store information. Knowing these are going to be crucial for recalling numbers. Perhaps you have heard or seen me do the demonstration where someone will give me a 100 digit number and I will recall it forwards, backwards, and by the number it was call out after. I did this, believe it or not, building up on the concepts we learned in the skeleton files. So everything we have learned up to this point is crucial and has a purpose.

The activities for today are simply to go back and read the activities we have completed each day and make sure you understand the lessons in each.

Counting in Japanese

You have learned a lot so far, but the fun is just beginning. As you will recall, anything can be a file system as long as there is more than one, and it goes in a logical order, and is something that you can use. Since these are the qualifications, our pencil list is actually going to be a file system for you just like the skeleton files and the city files are. So now, let's review the first 10 files on our pencil list. I chose to use the word file because that is exactly what they are going to be – places where we can store information. It could be lines of a poem or scripture, or as you will see later, we are going to learn a quote by Teddy Roosevelt very soon. Remember, that your mind thinks in pictures, and you must see these files in order to recall them.

Don't get bored that we are reviewing this file system again. I know that it may seem redundant, and at this point, I'll grant you it is, but please take my word for it – at this point is very necessary. We will get less and less redundant as we go along, and as you become more comfortable with this system. So don't give up now. You've invested too much time, and this is going to pay off in a big way for you. You will see what I mean as we go.

Number one, what is our file? It is a pencil. So get a clear picture in your mind of a pencil. Perhaps, it is a pencil holder on your desk, or a pencil sharpener, or a giant man-eating pencil with arms and legs. It doesn't matter what you see. The only stipulation is that you see a clear picture of a pencil, and it always is the same image that you are going to use for this file. For example, my number one file is a pencil holder on my desk.

What is your file for number 2? It's a sink. Get a very clear picture in your mind of a sink. It could be a kitchen sink, or a bathroom sink or a sink at your office. It doesn't matter, just see it, and make sure you always use the same one.

What is your number 3 file? It's circus. Get an image of a circus in your mind. What do you think of when you think of circus? Is it the tent, the elephants, the trapeze artists? Just see a circus and always use that image as your file.

Number 4, what's your file? It's a track. It could be a professional track at the Olympics, or a high school, or a college track, or even a racecar track. Just make sure every time you use the same track.

For number 5, what is our file? It's star. What do you think of when I say star? Is it the star on a flag, or maybe a night sky with the stars in the sky? Just see it.

Number 6, what is your file? It's bullet. Visualize the Lone Ranger's silver bullet, or one from an M16 – it doesn't matter. Just have a clear picture of a bullet in your mind's eye.

Number 7, what is your file? It is dice. Get an image of dice. Maybe it is a Monopoly board, or a craps table or another game. Just make sure it is always the same picture for dice.

What is your number 8 file? It's an hourglass. Get an image in your head. Maybe you have an hourglass on your table or desk. Once a man told me that when he thinks of an hourglass he sees his wife, because she has an hourglass figure. Whatever you see, it doesn't matter, just be consistent.

Number 9, what is your file? It is baseball. It could be a baseball player, a bat, a ball, a glove, a stadium…it doesn't matter. Just make it a clear picture and always use that same image for your file.

Number 10, what is your file? It's fingers. Now, this one will be pretty easy. It's familiar for all of us. Get an image of a hand in your mind.

We're going to stop there, but go back and review 11 through 20 when we wrap up for today and make sure you have pictures for all those numbers. Now, I am going to give you 10 pictures, and you are going to file these 10 pictures to your first 10 pencil list files. The files will be the pencil list and below are the 10 words. Remember move as fast as possible and test how fast you can memorize this list in the correct order.

1. Itching

2. Knee

3. Sun

4. Girl

5. Green traffic light

6. Fonzi (from 'Happy Days') in a row boat

7. The Sea and cheese (two word on this one)

8. Queso dip (hot melted cheese)

9. Fonzi (just the man)

10. Chew

Okay, now write down these 10 words in this exact order.

So, how did you do? Did you get a perfect score? If you did, give yourself a pat on the back. Now, if you didn't, ask yourself why? Did you know your file for each one? If you knew your file, and you were still unable to recall the information, it is because your picture was not vivid enough. Create a very strong image in your mind. If you see it, you will most likely not forget it. Now, before we wrap up our lesson for the day, what do you think that we just learned? We just learned to count to ten in Japanese!

one — **ichi**

two — **ni**

three — **san**

four — **shi**

five — **go**

six — **oku**

seven — **shichi**

eight — **hachi**

nine — **kyu**

ten — **ju**

1. Itching = Ichi

2. Knee = Ni

3. Sun = San

4. Girl = Shi (the pronoun she)

5. Green Traffic Light = Go

6. Fonzi in a row boat = Roku (ku is pronounced like cool and no one is cooler than Fonzi!)

7. Sea and cheese = Shichi

8. Hot cheese = Hachi

9. Fonzi = Ku (cool)

10. Chew = Ju

You can now count in Japanese! You may think that, "Well, that was no big deal, it was easy to learn! And you're right, it was. However, it was easy because we approached it from the correct angle the first time.

If you are a student who had to learn how to count in Japanese in less than 7 minutes, forwards and backwards by number, and you didn't have a memory system, I think that you would find it a daunting task. It was simple because of the system we used. However, as simple as it is, it is effective. Today, you learned a lot. It was a full lesson. So, take it in and pat yourself on the back for completing the lesson!

Memorizing Math Formulas

We're almost done building files. We are not going to review our skeleton files anymore. You have them at this point. If you don't, stop and make sure that you do. Before we begin filing anything to our body files, let me tell you two quick stories. Don't send these stories to files, just visualize them.

This is your first story: You have a huge globe in front of you. It is a 6-foot tall globe. As you stand in front of the globe notice that there are 7 continents, and some overlap into both the northern and southern hemisphere, but the majority of them are in the north. There are 4 in the northern hemisphere and 3 in the southern hemisphere. So, let's review. What is in front of you? A globe. How many continents in the north? Four. In the south? Three. Now, you notice a piece of a pie on top of the globe and you reach up to grab a piece of the pie, but just as soon as you do, you see a rat has been eating the pie, and you don't want to eat after a rat. He's at the North Pole, so he's frozen, or an ice cube. Right? Now, what was our picture? We had a globe, and how many continents in the north? Four. And what about the south? Three. What was on top of the globe? Pie. What was then next to the pie? A rat, and he was an ice cube. Now, move the picture off the screen of your mind. I'm going to give you a new picture.

Here is the second story: I want to introduce you to a friend of mine. He is a giant man-eating bumblebee from Texas. He is from Texas, so he is wearing a giant cowboy hat. Picture some parallel bars in your mind. This bee walks out with the hat and hops on the parallel bars and starts doing gymnastics. Now, if you saw that, you would never forget it, right? So picture it. Ok, now you have two stories in your mind that are actually pictures. What we did was take some abstract thoughts, which actually were calculus formulas, and we turned them into pictures and we then filed them to our files. Let me show you what I mean.

A stockbroker once attended my course in Austin, Texas. He was studying for his Series 7 test. He brought a book full of formulas. He had a lot of anxiety for the test, and was afraid he was not going to be able to recall the formulas. We approached them the exact way we approached these calculus formulas. What was the first story? It was about a globe, right? A globe is actually a sphere. So, the formula was to learn the volume formula for a sphere. The formula is: $sphere = 4/3\ r^2$. Each one of these items is an abstract thought, so we had to turn it into a picture. A globe for sphere, 4 continents in the north and 3 in the south, for 4/3. And a pie for the math symbol representing 3.14 (pi), a rat to represent r, and since the rat is an ice cube he represents cubed. That's pretty easy. Each item simply has to be turned into a picture to recall it, and then we created a story, just like the Mount Rainier story.

The stockbroker thought he was going to have to turn pictures for each formula, and that seemed like a daunting task for him. He didn't think there was any way. However, after looking at the formulas, he realized that the same symbols appeared in each formula over and over again. So, yes, he did have to turn each symbol into a picture, but he had to do it once. The next time he saw that symbol in an equation, he already had a picture for it. In calculus, r is a symbol that appears in a lot of formulas and stands for radius. So, if you are dealing with formulas, you only have to turn the variables into a picture once, the first time. Let's review the second formula quickly. It was the area formula for a parallelogram. The formula is written this way: parallelogram = bh, which means base times height. So, we had parallel bars for parallelogram; and a bee for b; and a cowboy hat for h. Pretty simple – Parallelogram = bh.

If you are a student, the applications are obvious. If you are a business professional, a concept is actually more important than the formulas. So, make sure you understand the concept. You just learned two calculus formulas whether you wanted to or not. And, remember it didn't seem like a challenge because we approached it from the correct angle the first time. If you are a student struggling to learn $4/3r^2$, and then you were given this memory system, I think you would appreciate it much more. So, be thankful that you didn't have to go through that to get the information.

Volume Formula

Sphere = $4/3\ \pi\ R^3$

Area

Parallelogram = BH
Circular Ring = $2\ \pi\ PW$

When recalling formulas, you must substitute a picture for the symbol or variable.

Math Symbol | Picture

Sphere = Globe

π (pi) = Piece of Pie

R (radius) = Rat

Parallelogram = Parallel Bars

B (base) = Bumble bee

H (height) = Hat

Circular Ring = Ring

P (perimeter) = Pirate

W (width) = Window

Creating Your House Files

What we are about to do is create some new files. These are my favorite files, and this is my favorite filing system. I use this file system 90% of the time, and I love them. What is it? It's called house files. We're going to use our homes as our filing system. It is very similar to the city files, the only difference is that instead of landmarks around our city, we will be using rooms, or areas of our house. This system will give us 25 files. After you complete this, you are going to have 10 skeleton files, 20 pencil list files, 10 city files, and 25 house files. That is 65 files. Sixty-five files will get most students through tests and most business professionals through product knowledge; information; training manuals; and other related items. On Day 15, we are actually going to learn how to build as many as 1,000 files. Can you believe that? I personally have about 2900 files. You are going to astound yourself at what your memory is capable of. Now, let's build those files!!

Select 5 rooms, or 5 sections in your house, and then in each of these 5 rooms, you're going to have 5 files. For example, your first room could be a bedroom, and you pick 5 pieces of furniture. The next room is the kitchen, and you pick 5 appliances. The next room is the bathroom, and you use 5 files, maybe the tub, toilet or sink. If you live in a small apartment, you still have 5 sections. A bathroom, a kitchen, a living room, a hall and a bedroom. If you need to use the front yard, parking lot, or driveway, do that. Just choose 5 sections.

After you have selected the 5 rooms or sections, then select 5 files in each room. Visualize yourself standing in the doorway of your first room. Then start at the right or the left, it doesn't matter, just so you're consistent. Then going clockwise or counterclockwise, choose 5 files. Pick big items over small items and spread them out across the room. In other words, don't cram all of your files on one side of the room. Spread them out evenly, and avoid using the same items in each room. For example, if you select a chair in one room, don't use a chair in the next. In review, select 5 rooms and 5 files in each room. If you use your front yard, then make one of the files a pole; another could be the grass, the mailbox, and so forth. Right now, make sure you have 5 rooms (or areas), and 5 files in each room. Later, if you have more room, feel free to add more files. Right now, keep it at 5 and 5. Don't put 6 files in one room and 4 in the next. The reason for that will make sense later.

Here is an example of what one of the rooms might look like:

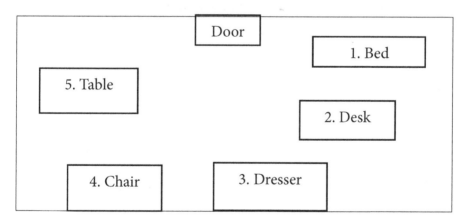

This is where you are going to store information. I just met a lady this week with an ERA real estate office. She took this course a few years ago. She was telling me how much she enjoyed the class, and she even took her son to the course. She said that when they moved her son said that they were not done packing. She looked at him like he was crazy. She said, "Of course we are!" He said, "No, Mom. I've still got my pictures hanging all over the files in the kitchen. I can't get them off. Every time I look in there, I see them." Now, that's a good imagination, and the kind we all need to have to make this system work. But don't worry, you can move, and even rearrange your furniture, because in your mind is where the files exist, and they stay the same in there.

I have created these mental journeys in every home I have ever lived in. I have also created journeys through my friend's homes. This will be a great exercise for you too. After you create your own house files I strongly encourage you to create a map like this of your family members' and friend's homes. You could easily create 200-300 files in just a few hours doing this.

Now for the instruction on how to do this: The first room is going to be one through 5, the second room is going to be 6 through 10, the third room is going to be 11 through 15, the fourth room is 16 through 20, and the fifth room is 21 through 25. The best thing that you can do right now is make sure you have these 25 files created, and review them until you know them cold, without hesitation, the number and the file.

Poems and Quotes

Welcome to Day 10. Did you enjoy building your house files yesterday? I hope so. I can't stress enough how much I like the house files, and how often I use them. As a matter of fact, we're going to use our house files right now! We are going to memorize a 20-line poem. That's right. We are going to learn a 20-line poem forwards, backwards and by number. Are you ready? First of all I would like you to read this poem through once or twice just to get a feel for it. Don't try to memorize it just now, simply read it and get a feel for it.

The Man in the Glass
By Dale Wimbrow

When you get what you want in your struggle for self

And the world makes you king for a day.

Just go to a mirror and look at yourself

And see what that man has to say.

For it is not your father, your mother or your wife

Whose judgment upon you must pass.

But the fellow's verdict who counts most in your life is the man

Looking back from the glass.

Some people may say you are a square-shooting chum

And call you a wonderful guy.

But the man in the glass says you're only a bum,

If you can't look him straight in the eye.

He is the one to please, never mind the rest,

For he's with you clear up until the end.

And you will pass your most dangerous and difficult test

If the man in the glass is your friend.

You may fool the whole world down the pathway of years

And get pats on your back as you pass.

But your final reward will be heartache and tears

If you've cheated the man in the glass.

That is a pretty powerful poem, isn't it? Every time I use it in a seminar, I always get quite a reaction. When memorizing a poem (or quotes, scripture, etc) we never turn every word into a picture. Instead, after reading each line or verse, we create a picture that will be a brain trigger for that line. I'm going to give you 20 pictures that you are going to file to your first 20 files. As we do this, look at each line of the poem that corresponds with the number. If you prefer to use your own pictures, then by all means, do that. Mine are just suggestions, but use what works for you. We are going to use our house files.

1. File two people who look exactly like you, and they are struggling or wrestling with each other.

2. Sitting on top of a globe with a king's crown on.

3. You – looking in a mirror

4. A man talking

5. Your mother, your father and your wife (or spouse, or what you would imagine they looked like if you had one!)

6. Judge in a car, and you are passing him

7. Jury foreman, standing up and giving a verdict on your life.

8. A man in a mirror looking back at you.

9. Gun that shoots square gum.

10. Jimmy Stewart from *It's A Wonderful Life*.

11. A mirror with a reflection of what you consider a bum to be. (For me, it is the 1954 Dodgers. People referred to them as bums.)

12. A huge eyeball that you can't stand to look at

13. Someone begging you please, if there are a lot of people behind him you pay no attention to the rest

14. A man running a race and crossing the finish line

15. Student passing a test

16. Your best friend in a glass

17. An old fool, walking down a pathway

18. Someone patting you on the back as you pass them

19. Someone handing you a trophy, and you start crying and your heart breaks

20. Stealing from the man in the glass

Now write down these 20 lines. Don't write the story necessarily, or the file, just the picture you saw. If you got stuck on one, don't worry about it. Move on to the next. We are not concerned with perfect scores. We are in the learning stage. So, stop now and fill in one through 20. DON'T try and write down the poem word for word, just the images that you saw. Later you can make sure the images are brain triggers for you for the poem.

Well, how did you do? Did you get 17 or more? If you did, that is very good. If you got a perfect score, that's even better! Now, remember, when you memorize scripture, or lines of a poem, you don't turn every single word into a picture. You simply use brain triggers, which are going to be cues for you. Remember that your mind works like a computer, and the glue must be strong for you. That is what holds the picture or data in place. The glue is the circuit board of your memory. Before we wrap up the lesson for the day, let's go through and review the poem, just so you are clear what the pictures represent.

Number one, two people struggling. The line of poetry is about when you get what you want in your struggle for self. Number two, a man sitting on top of a globe wearing a king's crown – "And the world makes you king for a day." Number 3, looking at your reflection in the mirror – "Just go to a mirror and look at yourself." Number 4 is a man talking – "And you see what that man has to say." Number 5 is your father, your mother, and your wife. The poem says, "For it is not your father, or your mother or your wife." Number 6, a judge passing you in a car. The poem says, "Whose judgment upon you must pass." Number 7 is a jury for man giving a verdict in your life. The poem says, "But the fellow's verdict who counts most in your life." Number 8 is a man's reflection in the mirror. The poem says, "Is the man looking back from the glass." Number 9 is a gun that shoots square gum, "Some people may call you a square-shooting chum." Number 10 is Jimmy Stewart in *It's A Wonderful Life*, "And call you a wonderful guy."

Number 11 is a mirror and your idea of what a bum looks like. The poetry says, "But the man in the glass says you're only a bum." Number 12 is a huge eye that you can't look straight at. The poetry says, "If you can't look him straight in the eye." Number 13 is someone with their hands folded, begging you please, with the rest of the people behind him. The poetry says, "For he is the one to please, never mind the rest." Number 14 is a runner crossing a finish line. The poetry says, "For he is with you clear up till the end." Number 15 is a student passing a test. The poem says, "You will pass your most dangerous and difficult test." Number 16 shows your best friend in a glass. The poem says, "If the man in the glass is your friend." Number 17 has an old fool walking down a pathway. The poetry says, "You may fool the whole world down the pathway of years." Number 18 has someone patting you on the back as you pass. The poem says, "And get pats on your back as you pass." Number 19 has someone handing you a trophy, and it breaks your heart and you start to cry. The poem says – "Your final reward will be heartache and tears." And, finally, number 20 – someone stealing from the man in the glass. The poem says – "If you have cheated the man in the glass." Wow! Do you realize what you just did? You just memorized a twenty-line poem forwards, backwards, and by number.

You might have to read the poem once or twice to fill in the blanks if the pictures don't make one hundred per cent sense to you. But give yourself some credit. I know that if you would have seen me looking at a poem for 5 minutes and then have been able to say the poem forwards, backwards, and by number, you would probably have been incredibly impressed with my memory. So, give yourself the same amount of credit that you would give me. You just accomplished something very remarkable. Soon, you will learn how to give speeches without notes and retain product knowledge. The skill you just learned is tremendous for lines of poetry, scriptures or quotations.

Memorizing Sales Presentations

Welcome back. It's Day 11. Have you been reciting *The Man in the Glass*? It is a great poem. It is extremely powerful. I conclude our workshop with it, and it is a powerful way to end this seminar. It really strikes a chord with some people. If you are a public speaker, this system will allow you to incorporate poems and quotations that draw your audience in. Also, I think it's a good point to remind you not to get caught up in being perfect.

You may have heard the story of Thomas Edison, about when he was constructing the light bulb. It took him over 1,000 attempts. After he successfully completed the light bulb, he held a press conference and a brash reporter asked him, "Mr. Edison, how does it make you feel to have failed over 1,000 times?" Mr. Edison without missing a beat, promptly responded, "You misunderstand. I did not fail over 1,000 times. I successfully found 1,000 ways the light bulb will not work." Now, that's a positive attitude. And it is an attitude that we can learn from for sure.

If you don't get a perfect score, do what Mr. Edison did. Ask yourself why. Learn something from the failure. Remember, you missed some for one of two reasons: It was either you didn't know your file, or your circuit board or action was not strong enough. Those are the only two reasons. So learn a lesson from Mr. Edison. The skill that I want to teach you next is how to give a sales presentation or, for that matter, any presentation without using notes. This is a moneymaking skill.

The filing system I use to give my presentation is my skeleton files. What are the skeleton files? Remember, they are top, nose, mouth, ribs, liver, joint, cap, fibula, ball and sand. This is where we are going to store a generic sales presentation. Let's say that you are a new salesperson, or even a veteran salesperson that would like to nail your presentation down a little better. What do you do? You break it down into separate thoughts, then turn those thoughts into pictures, and file them to your files. So, I'm going to give you 10 items and you need to scan through these very quickly. These items are going to represent the steps in a sales presentation. Most companies have a presentation that, at the end, has a call for action, and the presentation is designed in a very specific manner. There, most likely, is psychology behind the presentation, and all too often a salesperson will get caught up in the moment and forget the steps in his presentation, which weakens it. Your presentation may or may not be similar to the one we're about to learn, however, after you do this exercise you should have a very good understanding of a very practical business application to the system that we are learning.

File these pictures to your files **as fast as you can**. Make the pictures vivid and **KEEP MOVING!!**

1. Handshake for the introduction.

2. Statistics (to back up the value of your product)

3. Professional giving an opinion

4. Asking questions

5. Filling a need (what your product accomplishes)

6. Demonstration

7. Features and benefits

8. Testimonials, or third party references

9. Investment

10. Call to action

Okay, scan through it one more time if you have to, and then stop and write these 10 items down.

How did you do? If you got all 10 give yourself a pat on the back for a job well done. If you missed one, be sure to ask yourself why. Did you know your file and was your picture vivid enough? Give yourself some credit if you scored well. Remember that if you would have given me 10 pictures rapidly, and then I recited them back forwards, backwards, and by number, you would be very impressed. Well, guess what? That is what you just did. Now, for the practical application, this is what I use when I give my sales presentation. I file it to my skeleton files. If you were just learning a presentation or if you were a veteran, this will help you. You could even help a coworker learn this presentation.

Please keep in mind that not everyone is able to benefit from our training. When you see a young salesperson struggling to learn the steps of the presentation, tell him to build files in his office, and then use pictures as brain triggers. By the way, some of you may say, "Well, Ronnie, what if I file the 10 major points of my presentation, but there are details under each one that I can't recall? In this situation, what you would do is file the 10 major points, and then if there is more information that you want to file, place that on top. Go back and *layer* them on.

Remember, the Mount Rainier story taught us that we could link items and file them together. For example, we could file Mount Rainier to the top of your head right now, and we would actually have 19 items on that file. The principle is the same if you have more than one item to place to each file. Go back and layer them on top of one another. That is what I did for my sales presentation. After I was sure I had the 10 major points, I went back and filed minor points on top of the major ones. There you have it a sales presentation without notes!

Uses For Files

Now, let's learn a little bit about product knowledge. If you are a student, this will still apply to you because you can see how this will help you study for a test. I will show you as we go. We are going to use our house files for product knowledge. We have 5 rooms and 5 files in each room. In this scenario, you are going to be an automobile salesperson. However, this would work effectively if you sold copiers, homes, mortgages, insurance or something else. As a salesperson, you not only want to know the features and benefits of your product, you also want to know the benefits of similar models your competitors may have. This is the way to handle that. You dedicate your first room to the product knowledge about your merchandise.

Pick 5 key selling features of your product and file them to your files. Remember, we are going to use the example of you as an automobile sales professional for this one, so let's say you are a Toyota salesman focusing on sports utility vehicles. What you do is take the 5 selling features and file them to your first room. Perhaps it is legroom to one file, financing to another, sunroof to another. Whatever the 5 key selling features are, file them to your first 5 files. Now, you ask, "What are the next 4 rooms for?" Good question. I'm glad that you asked. Each one of these rooms is dedicated to your competition. That's right, you are going to dedicate a room of your house to your competitors. So, make room number two your Mazda room; room 3 your Jeep room; room 4 your Chevy room;

room 5 your Lincoln/Mercury room. Then in each one of these rooms list the 5 benefits your vehicles have over theirs. Be creative, and use your own imagination. If you sold copy machines one room could be your Xerox room; one your Panasonic room; and so on.

If you so desired you could fill up all 25 files with information on your product. The reason I throw in competition information is that people are comfortable doing business with the salesperson that knows a lot about the sales industry. This includes how their product measures up to the competition. If you are a student, you can use this same concept in studying for a test. Let's say you are taking a history test and you need to learn the major causes of the Civil War. You make one room your Civil War room, and you file the causes for the Civil War to that room. The next thing you might need to know is the major battles of the Civil War, so you file those in that room. The third room may be some important dates in the Civil War, and so on. This is just an example, however, you use the same concept as product knowledge. You can dedicate each room to a particular theme and then file information to that room. I recall studying for a psychology test one day, and in the first room I filed 5 major psychologists. The second room I used to file theories. The third room was for experiments, and I continued until I had all my notes on my files. For students, I would also encourage that you file rooms in your class. I remember when I was in school looking out the window, and the teacher would say, "Ronnie, the answer isn't on the window." Well, guess what? It might just be in this case. If you are a student, or a business professional, room files are a great way to group thoughts or ideas by room. It helps to organize them in your mind.

The activity today is going to be a little different. You know what situation you're in. Perhaps you need to recall product knowledge, or perhaps test information is more important to you. Use your house files if you are a salesperson who needs to file product knowledge to your files, just like we talked about. It may take a moment to sit down and actually do, however, even if you are veteran sales professional I think you will be astounded at the new information that you can store, even if it is about your competitors. If you are in the business arena, but not as a salesperson, then file information pertinent to your job. Perhaps it could be procedures or new training you are learning. If you are a student, this should be a "gimme". Get out your notes for your next test, and file them to your 25 house files. Remember that you can group them by room. Do it! And do not continue to the next lesson until you have done so. Remember that your final reward will be heartache and tears if you've cheated the man in the glass. So, don't cheat the man in the glass. Fill up your 25 files with something that is going to be a benefit to you and we will talk again tomorrow. Have a great day and get going!

Giving Speeches Without Notes

Welcome to Day 13. How did your exercises go yesterday? That was your first real test of something that you have to memorize every day. I'm confident that you found the room files very easy to use, and extremely helpful. So far we have filed information to our skeleton files, our house files, city files and the pencil list. These are all the files we are going to create together. So, at this point in the program, you have all the files that you are going to need to get through most everything. On Day 15, I will cover how to build up to 1,000 files. Yes, you heard that right, 1,000. Today, we are going to learn how to give speeches without the use of notes.

According to a survey that came out a few years ago, the number one fear in America is the fear of public speaking. The number two fear in that survey was the fear of death. Can you believe that? People are terrified of giving a speech. However, when you can give a speech without notes, it builds your credibility and your self-esteem. You are able to maintain eye contact, and the people you are talking to are impressed with your subject matter. They will notice when you aren't using notes. I instruct our live two-day seminars, and I never access a single note. That is 7 hours each day, and 14 hours total, and I never use a single note. Well, actually I'm using notes. I'm just that I am the only one who can see my notes. To instruct our seminars I take my notes, and then file them to my house files. I do not memorize my speech word-for-word. Imagine how boring that would be to listen to a speech that had been memorized word-for-word. Instead, I just file the major thoughts to my files and then jump from one file to the next in my mind. If you are called upon to give a speech, it will be most likely on a subject that you're familiar with, so you will not need to recall it word for word. Instead, you will use brain triggers to move from one file to the next. Let me show you whI'm going to give you 10 pictures and then you are to file these pictures to your house files. You are only going to use your first two rooms because I am going to give you 10 pictures. These 10 pictures are actually 10 items from a speech given on time management. Remember, we are going to use our house files, so sit back, relax, close your eyes, and think house files.

Here are the items. Memorize these as rapidly as you can! Try to just go through each word once and only a few seconds per word.

1. Clock

2. Organizer or day planner

3. "Things to do list"

4. Goal post to number 4

5. Cargo ship importing ants

6. Black jack dealer standing behind a gate

7. Fun

8. Calendar

9. Work room

10. Blueprints with glue

You know the drill, write these down and see how many that you get. Remember that you only need to write the picture down. Not the action or the files.

How did you do? Did you get all of them? If you didn't, remember that it's for only one of two reasons – either you didn't know your file, or your picture wasn't vivid enough. There is no other possible reason. When you give a speech without notes, you never memorize it word for word. Instead you have brain triggers to keep you moving from one thought to the next. What we have here are 10 brain triggers that will get us talking about ten major points. Follow along as I show you what I mean. This is a speech on time management.

You will open your speech with time management, which is why we filed the clock to the number 1 file. Remember that the code our mind uses to recall information is pictures, so we used a clock to represent time management. You used this brain trigger to introduce the subject of your speech to your audience.

The next thing that you talk about is filed to your number 2 file, an organizer or day planner. We want to talk about the word organized. After you see this prompt on your file, you can go into more depth with your audience, and perhaps talk with them about using a day timer or a Franklin planner, getting organized using a computer program, or simply a filing system at your office.

What is your number 3 file? What did you file to it, a "things to do list," right? Talk to your group about the importance of writing out a "Things to do list" every day. That way, you have a plan for the day, and your day does not simply happen around you.

Number 4 – what is your file? What did you file to it? A goal post, right? This represents the fact that you must set and establish goals to be organized. At this point you may mention the importance of setting goals with a deadline, and clearly define objectives.

Now, number 5, what did we file to number 5? Ants. Imported ants, right? This shows you the importance of words. You are importing ants. This is a mental cue to remind you that you need to place an importance on each item on your "things to do list," and make certain these items are a priority. Notice we are not memorizing every single word, just key words that are going to become brain triggers.

Number 6, what did we file to number 6? A black jack dealer behind a gate. The word we wanted to recall is delegate. We used a dealer for "del," and gate for "gate." So, we have delegate for number 6. This is important when you are assigning tasks for individuals and not trying to tackle the project on your own.

Number 7, what is your file? What did we file to it? We filed fun to that file. When you see this, remind your audience that it's important to set time aside for fun. All work and no play are not good, you must allocate time to let your mind relax and have some fun.

Number 8, what is your file? What did we file to it? You filed a schedule. When you see the schedule you'll remember that this is a brain trigger to talk about keeping a regular schedule, getting up at the same time every day, and keeping a routine. This will help you to use your time more wisely.

For number 9 you are going to talk about setting up a special room to work in. This is a place where you can go and get away from all distractions, and be able to focus on work.

We filed a blueprint with glue on it for number 10. That means that as you review your speech and recap the highlights, you want to reinforce your audience with the importance of having a plan and sticking to it. That is what the glue symbolizes. Sticking to it.

Now, you understand the concept of how to give a speech without notes. It is not important to memorize every word. Just make brain triggers and then file them to your files. Giving speeches without notes is an exclusive skill, and one that will increase your confidence when you master it. I encourage you to concentrate on this skill. It is a powerful one.

Foreign Languages

Welcome back. It's Day 14. How did you like learning how to give speeches without notes yesterday? That is a useful skill for business professionals, as well as students who are called on to give speeches in their class. I encourage you to go back and use this skill if you have to.

A lot of people want to learn foreign languages but don't know where to start. They will get on the treadmill and put on the foreign language tapes. Now this is better than nothing, but let's remind ourselves that our minds work like a computer, and we can use this to our benefit when we want to recall something. On Day 7, we learned how to count in Japanese. We did this by turning the first 10 numbers of Japanese into English pictures and then filed them to our pencil list. You could have just as easily substituted French numbers; German; Hebrew; or even Latin into pictures, and then file them to your files. Counting in a foreign language is not that hard at all when you approach it from the correct angle, and that angle would be to use our system. Focus, location, code, action and review

Here are some words that you don't see often:

Sire Nosh Morangu Pesagu Bosa Jontar Pie Puegas Payne Pastage

These are 10 words that are definitely not English. However, using the concept that our minds use the code of pictures to recall, we can very easily file these away. We are not going to actually stick these pictures on any of our organized file lists. Instead, we are going to file these pictures to their definitions. Follow along and you'll see what I mean.

The first word is sire. This is the Portuguese word for a woman's skirt. Visualize a woman's skirt sighing. It is a sire (sigh-er). You'll never forget that. The word is sire, and the definition is a woman's skirt.

The next word is the Portuguese word nosh, meaning walnut. Visualize yourself eating a giant walnut and it makes you nauseous. The word is nosh, and it means walnut.

The next word is morangu, and it means strawberry in Portuguese. See a gigantic strawberry eating a meringue pie. The word is morangu, and the definition is strawberry.

The next word is pesagu, and it is Portuguese for peach. See a giant peach asking you to pass the goo. That's right. A giant peach asking you to, "Pass the goo." The word is pesagu, and the definition is peach.

The next word is bosa, and it's Portuguese for a woman's purse. See a large piece of balsa wood carrying a woman's purse. You look out your window and you see a large piece of balsa wood carrying a woman's purse, that would be a picture that sticks in your mind. The word is bosa, and the Portuguese definition is purse.

The next word is jontar, and it is Portuguese for dinner. Now, file a man named John eating tar for dinner. A man named John, and he is eating tar for dinner. The word is jontar, and the definition is dinner.

The next word is pie and it is Portuguese for father. See yourself throwing a pie in your father's face. Hit your father in the face with a pie. The word is pie, and the definition is father.

The next word is puegas, and it is Portuguese for socks. Visualize some socks that have a really bad odor, and you say, "Phew, that smells like gas!" The word puegas, and the definition is socks.

The next word is pan, and it is French for bread. See a pan, and the handle is made of bread. The word is pan, and the definition is bread.

The final word is pastake. Pastake is French for watermelon. See a watermelon passing a deck of cards to you. The word is pastake, and the definition is watermelon.

As you can see, learning a foreign language is very simple. You must turn it into a picture, and then file it to its definition. Any word can be turned into a picture, or something can be substituted for it. You have just learned a little bit of French and Portuguese! Can you believe that? It was pretty painless, wasn't it?

Let's see how many definitions that you can recall now. Fill in the blanks below with the definitions:

1. Saia _____

2. Noz _____

3. Morangoo _____

4. Passego _____

5. Bolsa _____

6. Jantar _____

7. Pai _____

8. Peugas _____

9. Pain _____

10. Pasteque _____

So, how did you do? Did you get all of them? If you didn't, ask yourself why. Was your picture vivid enough? The code your mind thinks in is pictures, and you must make the pictures very strong. I do want you to understand that this concept we just learned for foreign language can also be used for English words. Have you ever learned words that are new to you? Sure you have. Even in English, I would dare say, there are many words that in some fashion or form are foreign to you. Use the same concept that we used for foreign languages. For example, take the word neophyte. It's an English word. It means beginner. What if you saw a boxing match or a fight and the boxers were on their knees? That would be a knee fight, wouldn't it? We turn the word into a picture, and the word is beginner. Say we have the audience as a bunch of bees, and they're drinking gin. It's a knee fight with bees drinking gin. That is a picture that you wouldn't forget even if you tried. Make it a goal of yours to learn a foreign language, or expand upon the one you already know. Purchase an audio program or a book, and learn a few words a day or a week with this method. At the end of the year, I think you'll be impressed with your vocabulary. And remember this quote that I live by, "A year from now you will have wished you started today." So, seize the day with your newly found skills.

Intro to Number Memory

Welcome back. It's Day 15. Are you bilingual yet? Well, you'll get there if it is a goal of yours and you put this system into practice. You will amaze yourself if you do everything your mind is capable of doing. What we are about to learn now is a very useful skill. I find that it is so useful, that I'm going to spend 3 days on it. I hope you are ready to really expand your memory capabilities. This is going to be a skill that if you master it, you will astound people with your memory.

I'm going to show you how to memorize a 100-digit number after just hearing it once! On March 7th, 2009 I actually memorized a 167-digit number in 5 minutes to set a new USA record. When my friends get bored, they will write out a series of numbers and I will do this demonstration. It never fails to get quite a reaction. However, it is very simple, and it is also very useful. I use this skill to memorize phone numbers. When I was a student, I used to recall dates and other important numbers. This is somewhat an advanced skill; so don't worry if it doesn't make 100% sense the first time. This is something that you may have to review 3 or 4 times to understand the concept.

What are the 5 things that you need to memorize something, or anything? They are focus, location, code, action and review. When recalling a number, the location is no problem. We could use our house files, skeleton files, city files or even the pencil list. The challenge is the code or the pictures. Numbers are abstract and must be turned into a picture before we can recall them. We turned items one through 20 into pictures using basic association on the pencil list. However, it is sometimes hard to think of an association for every number. For example, what is an association for 86? That would be a challenge, and most likely require some thought. What if I told you that there's a system to turning numbers into pictures. That's right – there is a system! This is not a new system at all. It has been around for quite some time.

This system was actually introduced more than 300 years ago, by Stonsen Mink Vonwesenhein. Vonwesenhein's basic construction was modified by Dr. Richard Gray, an Englishman. The major system was devised to allow the master memorizers of the time to break the bonds of previously excellent, but more limited systems. This system was developed to memorize long digit numbers.

For every number from zero to 9 a consonant sound is assigned to that letter. The sounds have been assigned to these numbers for hundreds of years, since Dr. Richard Gray. Here they are:

0 = Suh

1 = Tuh

2 = Nuh

3 = Muh

4 = Ruh

5 = Luh

6 = Juh

7 = Kuh

8 = Fuh

9 = Buh

All you have to do is memorize these. Does that sound like a challenge?

What if I told you that I bet you could learn these in less than a minute? What if I told you that you have already memorized them? That's right, you've already memorized these. I already taught them to you. Remember when I told you that everything in this course is done for a reason, and I'm actually going to teach you things that you are not even using yet? Well, here's an example of that. Remember when we learned our skeleton files? Let's review what our files were. Top, nose, mouth, ribs, liver, joint, cap, fibula, ball and sand. Now, let's review the phonic sounds. They are tuh, nuh, muh, ruh, luh, shuh, juh, cuh, fuh, puh or buh and suh. Did you catch that? Let's go slow this time. The consonant sound assigned to number one is tuh, and the first skeleton file is top. So number one is "t" that has the tuh sound. The letter assigned to number two is "n" because it has the nuh sound and the second skeleton file is nose. So number two is "n" for nuh. The letter assigned to the number 3 is "m" and our third skeleton file is mouth. Number three is "m". The letter assigned to four is ruh. The fourth skeleton file is ribs. Number 4 is ruh, or "r." Four is represented by "r" or ruh. The fifth skeleton file is liver, and the letter assigned to number five is "l." Five is "l" or luh. That is easy enough, isn't it?

However, once you get this down, it's going to catapult your memory to the expert memory level. The letter assigned to 6 is juh or shuh and the sixth skeleton file is joint. Joint represents the "j" or juh. The letter assigned to your seventh file is a hard "c" sound or "k" – kuh. And the seventh skeleton file is cap, so file number7 is a hard "c" or a "k." The letter assigned to the number 8 is "f" or "v." Your eighth skeleton file is "f" or "v." Your eighth skeleton file is your fibula. Number eight is "f" or "v," or fuh or vuh. The letter assigned to your number 9 is puh or buh, "p" and "b." And your ninth skeleton file is ball. So number 9 is "p" or "b." And finally, the last skeleton file is actually number 10, but for the purposes of this system, this will represent the number zero. Zero is assigned to a soft "c" or "s." Zero is the suh sound.

The 10 primary phonetic sounds are tuh, nuh, muh, ruh, luh, shuh, juh, kuh, fuh, puh or buh and suh. Stop now to review your skeleton files and make sure that you know the sounds one through 10, where 10 is actually representing zero. Make sure that you know them.

Here are a few examples of how you would use this system to turn numbers into pictures. Remember we only add vowels.

Number | Phonetic Sound | Picture

35 | 3 = M 5 = L | MaLL

72 | 7 = C 2 = N | CaN

59 | 5 = L 9 = P | LaP

25 | 2 = N 5 = L | NaiL

Now you try:

Number | Phonetic Sound | Picture

17 | 1 = 7 = | _____

47 | 4 = 7 = | _____

79 | 7 = 9 = | _____

24 | 2 = 4 = | _____

14 | 1 = 4 = | _____

83 | 8 = 3 = | _____

56 | 5 = 6 = | _____

38 | 3 = 8 = | _____

49 | 4 = 9 = | _____

95 | 9 = 5 = | _____

82 | 8 = 2 = | _____

55 | 5 = 5 = | _____

45 | 4 = 5 = | _____

77 | 7 = 7 = | _____

29 | 2 = 9 = | _____

So, how did you do? Does this take some getting used to? You better believe it! Have you ever turned numbers into pictures this way before? I bet not. If it seems a little bit unusual to you, don't worry about it! However, you most likely never have attempted to memorize a 100-digit number before. To do something you have never done before, you must learn things that you have never learned before.

Here are my pictures for numbers 1-100.

1 – Hat	17 – Tack	33 – Mom
2 – Hen	18 – Dove	34 – Mare
3 – Ham	19 – Top	35 – Mall
4 – Hair	20 – Nose	36 – Match
5 – Hail	21 – Net	37 – Mug
6 – Hash	22 – Nun	38 – Muff
7 – Hook	23 – Name	39 – Mop
8 – Ivy	24 – Nero	40 – Rice
9 – Hoop	25 – Nail	41 – Rat
10 – Ties	26 – Notch	42 – Rain
11 – Dot	27 – Neck	43 – Ram
12 – Tin (can)	28 – Knife	44 – Rear
13 – Dime	29 – Nap	45 – Roll
14 – Tire	30 – Mice	46 – Rash
15 – Tile	31 – Mat	47 – Rock
16 – Dish	32 – Moon	48 – Roof

49 – Rope	69 – Ship	89 – Fob
50 – Lice	70 – Case	90 – Bus
51 – Light	71 – Cat	91 – Pot
52 – Lane	72 – Can	92 – Pan
53 – Lame	73 – Comb	93 – Bum
54 – Lure	74 – Car	94 – Pour
55 – Lily	75 – Coal	95 – Pool
56 – Leash	76 – Cash	96 – Bush
57 – Lock	77 – Kicking	97 – Pack
58 – Leaf	78 – Cough	98 – Puff
59 – Lap	79 – Cap	99 – Pipe
60 – Juice	80 – Face	100 – Doses
61 – Jet	81 – Fat	
62 – Shin	82 – Fan	
63 – Gym	83 – Foam	
64 – Jar	84 – Fire	
65 – Jail	85 – File	
66 – Judge	86 – Fish	
67 – Shack	87 – Fog	
68 – Chef	88 – Fife (Barney)	

For numbers 1-9 I use the letter "H" because it is a silent consonant sound, and it helps if you have more than one consonant when creating a word so the letter "H" helps us out here. Also it is important to note that the following phonetic sounds share a number:

1 = tuh or duh

6 = shuh or juh

7 = kuh or guh

8 = fuh or vuh

9 = puh or buh

If you move your mouth to make the sounds puh and buh you will see that your mouth moves in the same way. These are phonetically the same. The same is true with the other sounds listed above. This gives you more options when creating pictures for numbers.

There is also another method for creating pictures for numbers, and this method is referred to as "Character/Action." The idea or concept behind this method is that you use a person or character for each number. My character for 88 is Michael Irvin, the former wide receiver for the Dallas Cowboys, because his number was 88. The action for 88 for me is receiving a pass.

The challenge with this is that if you are simply looking at each number it can be difficult to think of a person or character that this number reminds you of. That is where the method above for having letters for numbers actually helps. Let's take 77. That is Kuh Kuh. So my character for 77 is "King Kong," and the action is climbing a building.

Let's do one more, the number 24 is Nuh and Ruh. So my person for 24 is Chuck Norris, and the action is a karate kick. You can create your own rules here for this method. You can use the letters "N" and "R" as initials or sounds of the last name. It is your system so make your own rules!

With this character/action method you can actually recall 4 digits at a time. Let's take the number 7724. For the first pair of digits use the character and for the second pair of digits you use the action. So 77 would be King Kong and 24 would be a karate kick. You have King Kong delivering a karate kick!

The number 2488 would be Chuck Norris for 24 and receiving a pass for 88. The first set of numbers is the person, and the second the action. If you wanted to take it one step further you could develop an object to go with the character/action. The object for 24 could be a board (karate kicking a board), the object for 88 could be a football (catching a football). If you did this you could memorize 6 digits at a time! This is the method I used when I set the USA record for most numbers memorized in 5 minutes (167 consecutive digits)

Make sure that you understand Day 15 completely (100%) before moving on to Day 16.

How to Memorize Numbers

We are going to go a little more in depth with phonics today. The best way to practice phonics is every time you hear a number, turn it into a picture. You are going to encounter numbers tomorrow anyway, so you might as well turn them into a picture. When you are driving today, you are going to see an exit sign that will say Exit 56. Turn that into a picture. Say to yourself, 5 is luh, and 6 is shuh, so luh and shuh, it's a leash! Whammo, you have just turned 56 into a picture! You may say, "Ronnie, that's a lot of work, and I'm going to have to do that every time I want to remember a number?" Absolutely not! You are going to have to do that the first time only. The next time you run across 56, you've already turned it into a picture.

Initially, you are going to have to go through the steps when you want to turn 56 into a picture. However, the next time the work is already done. When I hear numbers today, I am no longer turning them into a picture. I already have the pictures.

I'm going to give you 35 pictures and you are going to file them to your house files for 1-25, and your skeleton files for 26-35. Each one of these pictures is representative of a number.

I encourage you to set a timer for 5 minutes for this next exercise. If you finish before the 5 minutes is up GREAT, if not do your best to finish in 5 minutes. You will have memorized a 70-digit number in 5 minutes if you do this. Currently, the United States record is 160-digits in 5 minutes, but 70 digits are VERY respectable. Don't beat yourself up if you don't get them all, but let's shoot for it.

Here are the words. Place 1-25 on your house files, and 26-35 on your skeleton files.

1. Nail	14. Dove	26. Rat
2. Can	15. Cat	27. Pan
3. Juice	16. Pipe	28. Pack
4. Moon	17. Dish	29. Nap
5. Mall	18. Shin	30. Leash
6. Match	19. Tire	31. Mall
7. Bus	20. Fish	32. Jar
8. Tin	21. Jet	33. File
9. Fire	22. Rat	34. Leaf
10. Chef	23. Mom	35. Shack
11. Mop	24. Foam	
12. Pool	25. Case	
13. Ship		

Now, stop and write these words out 1-35.

You just memorized a 70-digit number! Here it is:

1. Nail = 25	19. Tire = 14
2. Can = 72	20. Fish = 86
3. Juice = 60	21. Jet = 61
4. Moon = 32	22. Rat = 41
5. Mall =35	23. Mom = 33
6. Match =36	24. Foam = 83
7. Bus = 90	25. Case = 70
8. Tin = 12	26. Rat = 41
9. Fire = 84	27. Pan = 92
10. Chef = 68	28. Pack = 97
11. Mop = 39	29. Nap = 29
12. Pool = 95	30. Leash = 56
13. Ship = 69	31. Mall = 35
14. Dove = 18	32. Jar = 64
15. Cat = 71	33. File = 85
16. Pipe = 99	34. Leaf = 58
17. Dish = 16	35. Shack = 67
18. Shin = 62	

How did you do? Perfect score? Did you get close? This is fun, isn't it? One important note for numbers starting with 0, we don't have images for 09, 08, 07, etc. Remember 0 is the 'suh' sound. So for 07 it is suh and kuh. My picture for 07 is sack. Go ahead and create your own images for the digits starting with 0 – and enjoy!

Pictures for Numbers to 1000

Turning numbers into pictures has many practical applications. It is great for remembering phone numbers, product knowledge, technical data, product codes and more. Personally, I have used this method to turn every number between 1 and 1000 into a picture. The sounds for 127 are 'tuh', 'nuh' and 'kuh'. Therefore my picture for 127 is a tank.

Here are my pictures for every number up to 1000!

101 – Toast	110 – Tights	119 – Tadpole
102 – Dozen	111 – Dotted	120 – Tennis
103 – Decimal	112 – Titanic	121 – Tent
104 – Dessert	113 – Totem (pole)	122 – Tenant
105 – Diesel	114 – Theater	123 – Dynamite
106 – Dosage	115 – State line	124 – Diner
107 – Desk	116 – Hot dish	125 – Tunnel
108 – Adhesive (tape)	117 – Tie tack	126 – Dungeon
109 – Teaspoon	118 – Tooth filling	127 – Tank

128 – Tinfoil

129 – Tin pan

130 – Damsel

131 – Tomato

132 – Diamond

133 – Teammate

134 – Timer

135 – Oatmeal

136 – Time sheet

137 – Tomahawk

138 – Steam fitter

139 – Dimple

140 – Trees,

141 – Turtle

142 – Train

143 – Trampoline

144 – Dryer

145 – Drill

146 – Trash

147 – Truck

148 – Trophy

149 – Tripod

150 – Tails

151 – Toilet

152 – Talon

153 – Toll man

154 – Tailor

155 – Taillight,

156 – Tool shed

157 – Telegram

158 – Telephone

159 – Tulip

160 – Dishes

161 – Touchdown

162 – Station

163 – Taj Mahal

164 – T-shirt

165 – Dash light

166 – Head judge

167 – Stagecoach

168 – Dish full

169 – Tissue paper

170 – Taxi

171 – Ticket

172 – Token

173 – Document

174 – Tiger

175 – Tackle

176 – Dictionary

177 – Digging

178 – Takeoff (airplane)

179 – Teacup

180 – Thieves

181 – Divot

182 – Typhoon

183 – TV man

184 – Diver

185 – Devil

186 – Hot fudge

187 – Stuffing

188 – Dive off

189 – Stove pipe

190 – Tubes, tubs

191 – Teapot

192 – Headband

193 – Topmast

194 – Typewriter

195 – Table

196 – Top shelf

197 – Top Coat

198 – Deep Freeze

199 – Hot pepper

200 – Noses

201 – Nest

202 – Ensign

203 – Newsman

204 – Newsreel

205 – Nozzle

206 – Incision

207 – Unicycle

208 – News vendor

209 – Newspaper

210 – Nudist

211 – Handout

212 – Antenna

213 – Ointment

214 – Internet

215 – Noodle

216 – Nutshell

217 – Nightgown

218 – Native

219 – Notebook

220 – Onions

221 – Noontime (face of Clock)

222 – Neon nest

223 – Onion meal

224 – Onion ring

225 – Union hall

226 – Union Jack (Flag)

227 – Nanny goat

228 – Neon foot

229 – Neon pins

230 – Gnomes

231 – Inmate

232 – Honeymoon (Niagara Fall)

233 – New member (club)

234 – Numeral

235 – Animal

236 – Animation (cartoon)

237 – New microphone

238 – Nymph

239 – Nameplate

240 – Nurse

241 – Narrator

242 – No running (sign)

243 – Unarmed

244 – Honorary (degree)

245 – one-reel

246 – Nourishment (food)

247 – New York

248 – Nerve

249 – Unwrap (sandwich)

250 – Nails

251 – Unload

252 – Nylon

253 – Newly made (fresh Bread)

254 – Inhaler

255 – Nail hole

256 – Unleash (dog)

257 – Nail cup

258 – Nail file

259 – Nail polish

260 – Notches

261 – Unshod

262 – Engine

263 – in gym

264 – Insurance (policy)

265 – Enchilada

266 – Hinge joint

267 – Inject (needle)

268 – Unshaven

269 – Hunchback

270 – Yankees

271 – Nugget

272 – Noggin (head)

273 – Honeycomb

274 – Anchor

275 – Nickel

276 – Engagement (ring)

277 – Necking

278 – New calf

279 – Innkeeper

280 – Knives

281 – Nevada (Las Vegas)

282 – Infantry

283 – Navy man

284 – University

285 – Navel

286 – Navy ship

287 – Navigator

288 – Knife fight

289 – Navy Pier

290 – Knobs

291 – Neptune

292 – Knee band

293 – Napalm (bomb)

294 – Neighbor

295 – Napoleon

296 – Nuptials (marriage Ceremony)

297 – Napkin

298 – Unpaved

299 – Nabob

300 – Moses

301 – Moustache

302 – Messenger

303 – Museum

304 – Masseur

305 – Missi306 – Massage

307 – Musket

308 – Mice food

309 – Misprint

310 – Maids

311 – Matador

312 – Mitten

313 – Madam

314 – Mtere

315 – Motel

316 – Midshipman (at Annapolis)

317 – Medical (student)

318 – Mid-field (50-yard line)

319 – Meatball

320 – Mayonnaise

321 – Mint

322 – Manhunt

323 – Monument

324 – Miner

325 – Moonlight

326 – Manager

327 – Mannequin

328 – Manifold (engine)

329 – Money bags

330 – Mummies

331 – Mammoth

332 – Memento

333 – Mamma Mia

334 – Mom reads

335 – Mammal

336 – Mom shouts

337 – M&M Candy

338 – Home movie

339 – Mumps

340 – Mare saddled

341 – Martini

342 – Marine

343 – Mermaid

344 – Mirror

345 – Mural

346 – Martian

347 – Marker

348 – Moor fight

349 – Marble

350 – Mills (fabric mills)

351 – Mullet

352 – Melon

353 – Mailman

354 – Molar (tooth)

355 – Molehill

356 – Mulch

357 – Milk

358 – Mile face

359 – Mailbag, mailbox

360 – Matches

361 – Machete

362 – Mission

363 – Matchmaker

364 – Mushroom

365 – Match holder

366 – Magician

367 – Mashing

368 – Home chef

369 – Matchbook

370 – Hammocks

371 – Macadamia (nut)

372 – Mechanic

373 – Homecoming

374 – Microscope

375 – Mogul (skiing)

376 – Mug shot

377 – Home cooking

378 – Megaphone

379 – Makeup

380 – Movies

381 – Amphitheater

382 – Muffin

383 – Movie maker

384 – Mover

385 – Mayflower (pilgrims), Muffler

386 – Movie show

387 – Movie camera

388 – Mafia family

389 – Movie pilot

390 – Embassy

391 – Amputee

392 – Embankment

393 – Map maker

394 – Umpire

395 – Maple (syrup),

396 – Ambush

397 – Hymnbook

398 – Mop face

399 – Humpback (whale)

400 – Roses

401 – Roast

402 – Raisin

403 – Horseman

404 – Razor

405 – Wrestle

406 – Horseshoe

407 – Race course	430 – Arms	452 – Airline
408 – Receiver	431 – Hermit	453 – Heirloom
409 – Raspberry	432 – Roman	454 – Roller
410 – Roadster	433 – Roommate	455 – Whale Oil
411 – Redhead	434 – Armory	456 – Relish
412 – Red nose	435 – Airmail	457 – Relic
413 – Radioman	436 – Armchair	458 – Airlift
414 – Radar	437 – Arm guard	459 – Earlobe
415 – Radial	438 – Earmuff	460 – Ridges
416 – Radish	439 – Ramp	461 – Ratchet
417 – Red coat	440 – Errors (baseball),	462 – Russian
418 – Artifact (fossil)	441 – Reward (sign)	463 – Rushmore (Mount)
419 – Redbreast (Robin)	442 – Warranty	464 – Rush hour
420 – Rhinoceros	443 – Re-warm	465 – Ritual
421 – Hornet	444 – Rear horse (race)	466 – Rush job
422 – Reunion (class)	445 – Rear alley	467 – Reject
423 – Rain Main (movie)	446 – Worship (church)	468 – Hair shave
424 – Runner	447 – Rear-guard	469 – Airship
425 – Rain, hail	448 – Rear view (mirror)	470 – Rugs
426 – Ranch	449 – Hair rope	471 – Rocket
427 – Rank	450 – Rails	472 – Reagan (Ronald)
428 – Rainforest	451 – Roulette	473 – Rug man
429 – Rainbow		474 – Rocker

475 – Regular

476 – Air gauge

477 – Rock cliff

478 – Rock fall

479 – Rugby

480 – Harvest

481 – Raft

482 – Orphan

483 – Roof man

484 – Roofer

485 – Rifle

486 – Refugee

487 – Ref Call

488 – Revival

489 – Wave Pool

490 – Ribs

491 – Robot

492 – Ribbon

493 – Air bomb

494 – Robber

495 – Ripple

496 – Rubbish

497 – Reebok (Shoe)

498 – Repave

499 – Rope Bull

500 – Lazy Susan

501 – Holster

502 – Lozenge

503 – Wholesome

504 – Lizard

505 – Lysol

506 – Yellow sachet

507 – Alaska (baked)

508 – Lucifer (devil)

509 – Lace pajamas

510 – Llighthouse

511 – Low tide

512 – Lightning

513 – Altimeter

514 – Ladder

515 – Ladle

516 – Late show

517 – Lithograph

518 – lead-off
(baseball)

519 – Ladybug

520 – Aliens

521 – Island

522 – Linen

523 – Lineman

524 – Liner (baseball),

525 – Linoleum

526 – Lingerie

527 – Lincoln (Abe)

528 – Lion family

529 – Line-up

530 – Limousine

531 – Helmet

532 – Lemon

533 – Alma mater

534 – Hallmark

535 – Oil hill

536 – Limejuice

537 – Lamb kills

538 – Lamb face

539 – Lamp

540 – Lawyers

541 – Lard

542 – Lure net

543 – Alarm

544 – Lure watch

545 – Laurel (wreath)

546 – Allergy
(sneezing)

547 – Lark (bird)

548 – Larva

549 – Lure bag

550 – Lilies

551 – Hall Light

552 – Lowland

553 – Oil lamp

554 – Lily wedding

555 – Low lily

556 – Low latch

557 – Lilac

558 – Yellow liver

559 – Lollipop

560 – Latches, lodges

561 – Lodged

562 – Lotion

563 – Hall chime

564 – Ledger

565 – Oil shale

566 – Ill judge

567 – Latchkey

568 – Low shaft

569 – Oil ship

570 – Legs

571 – Locket

572 – Lagoon

573 – Locomotive

574 – Locker

575 – Legal

576 – Luggage

577 – Leggings

578 – Lake front, alcove

579 – Helicopter

580 – Leaves, loaves, olives

581 – Lift

582 – Elephant

583 – Leaf man

584 – Lever

585 – Level

586 – Live Show

587 – Lifeguard

588 – Laughing

589 – Lifeboat

590 – Lips

591 – Halibut

592 – Albino

593 – Album

594 – Librarian

595 – Label

596 – Hill Bush

597 – Law book

598 – Leapfrog

599 – Oil pipe

600 – Cheeses

601 – Chest

602 – Chasing

603 – Chessman

604 – Juicer

605 – Chisel

606 – Cheese shop

607 – Cheesecake

608 – Juice vat

609 – Cheeseburger

610 – Shades

611 – Shaded

612 – Shut-in

613 – Showtime

614 – Ashtray

615 – Shuttle

616 – Judiciary (Supreme Court)

617 – Shotgun

618 – Shut off (water)

619 – Shot put

620 – Oceans

621 – Giant

622 – Chain noose

623 – Chain male

624 – Shiner

625 – Channel

626 – Chinchilla

627 – Junk

628 – Ocean front

629 – Chin up, shin bone

630 – Gems

631 – Gummed

632 – Chimney

633 – Jam maker

634 – Shamrock

635 – Gemologist

636 – Gym shoe

637 – Shoemaker

638 – Jam full

639 – Chimp

640 – Cherries

641 – Chariot

642 – Journal

643 – German

644 – Juror

645 – Cheerleader

646 – Charge

647 – Shark

648 – Giraffe

649 – Cherry pie

650 – Jailhouse

651 – Gelatin

652 – Chow line

653 – Jail man

654 – Jewelry

655 – Shell hole

656 – Jail shade

657 – Chalk

658 – Jellyfish

659 – Jailbird

660 – Judges

661 – judged (condemned Man)

662 – Shoe shine

663 – Judgment (day)

664 – Cheshire cat

665 – Judge lawyers

666 – Judge showdown

667 – Judge kids

668 – Shoe shuffling

669 – Shoe shop

670 – Cheeks

671 – Jacket

672 – Chicken

673 – Jackhammer

674 – Joker

675 – Chocolate

676 – Ejection

677 – Jockey kick

678 – chock-full (of nuts)

679 – Checkbook

680 – Chefs

681 – Shaft

682 – Chiffon

683 – chief-mate (Navy)

684 – Chauffeur

685 – Javelin

686 – Chef show

687 – Chef cake

688 – Shave off (a beard)

689 – Chef bakes

690 – Chaps

691 – Chapter (book)

692 – Jawbone

693 – Chipmunk

694 – Shipwreck

695 – Shoplifter

696 – Egyptian

697 – Shopkeeper

698 – Shop Lifter

699 – Ship builder

700 – Kisses

701 – Cassette

702 – Cousin

703 – Casement

704 – Geyser

705 – Gasoline

706 – Quiz show

707 – Casket

708 – Goose foot

709 – Gazebo

710 – Kites

711 – Cathedral

712 – Cotton

713 – Catamaran

714 – Guitar

715 – Cattle

716 – Cottage

717 – Catacomb

718 – Catfish

719 – Octopus

720 – Gunnysack

721 – Candle

722 – Cannon

723 – Gunman

724 – Canary

725 – Kennel

726 – Gunshot (wound)

727 – Eggnog

728 – Convict

729 – Canopy

730 – Chemist

731 – Comet

732 – Commander

733 – Comb, men

734 – Camera

735 – Camel

736 – Gumshoe

737 – Kamikaze

738 – Camouflage

739 – Camp

740 – Corsage

741 – Cardinal

742 – Carnation

743 – Aquarium

744 – Courier

745 – Corral

746 – Crutch

747 – Cork

748 – Graffiti

749 – Crab

750 – Gallows

751 – Kilt

752 – Gallon

753 – Column

754 – Caller

755 – Galley

756 – College

757 – Calk

758 – Cauliflower

759 – Caliper

760 – Coaches

761 – Caged

762 – Cushion

763 – Cashmere

764 – Catcher

765 – Eggshell

766 – Cash, shoe

767 – Cash Cow

768 – Cash fire

769 – Ketchup

770 – Quicksand

771 – Cactus

772 – Coconut

773 – Cucumber

774 – Cockroach

775 – Google

776 – Cowcatcher

777 – Cake, cover

778 – Kickoff (Football)

779 – Cookbook

780 – Caves

781 – Cavity

782 – Coffin

783 – Cave man

784 – Gopher

785 – Gavel

786 – Coffee shop

787 – Coffee cup

788 – Coffee field

789 – Coffee pot

790 – Cowboys

791 – Cupid

792 – Cabin

793 – Cab man

794 – Copper

795 – Cable

796 – Cabbage

797 – Cupcake, hockey puck

798 – Cupful

799 – Copyboy, kabob (shish)

800 – Faces, fuses, vases

801 – Faucet

802 – Pheasant

803 – Face Make up

804 – Officer

805 – Vaseline

806 – Physician

807 – Physique (body builder)

808 – Face-off (hockey)

809 – Vice President, Office boy

810 – Fights, footstool, vats

811 – Faded (blue jeans)

812 – Footnote, evidence (Trial)

813 – Fat man, vitamin

814 – Father, feather, Veterinarian

815 – Fiddle, footlocker

816 – Food show

817 – Vodka, photograph

818 – Photo finish

819 – Football, footpath, Footprint

820 – Fence, fins, vines

821 – Fountain

822 – Phone Nokia

823 – Venom

824 – Vineyard

825 – Funnel

826 – Finish (line)

827 – Vinegar

828 – Fanfare

829 – Fan Belt

830 – Foams

831 – Foam hat

832 – Half-moon

833 – Foam mouth

834 – Femur

835 – Family

836 – Famished

837 – Fumigate

838 – Family Fun

839 – Fumble

840 – Firehouse

841 – Fruit

842 – France

843 – Fireman

844 – Forearm

845 – Overalls

846 – Fresh

847 – Frog

848 – Forefinger

849 – Fireplace

850 – Fleece (sheep)

851 – Flood

852 – Flannel

853 – Flamingo

854 – Flare

855 – Fuel oil

856 – Flesh

857 – Volcano

858 – velvet

859 – Flap

860 – Fishes, vichyssoise

861 – Fishtail

862 – Fashion (show)

863 – Fish mouth

864 – Voucher

865 – Fish oil

866 – Fish jaw

867 – Fishhook

868 – half-shaved

869 – Fishbowl

870 – Figs,

871 – Factory, avocado

872 – Afghan

873 – Vacuum

874 – Foghorn

875 – Focal

876 – Vacation

877 – Half-cocked (gun)

878 – ivy-covered

879 – Fig bowl

880 – Fives (High Fives)

881 – Five toes

882 – View finder

883 – Five men

884 – Favor (party)

885 – half-oval

886 – Five shoes

887 – Five Kids

888 – Five fingers

889 – Five pins (bowling)

890 – Fobs (watch)

891 – Half a bat (baseball)

892 – half pint (ice cream)

893 – Fob maker (Watch maker)

894 – Fabric

895 – Feeble (old man)

896 – Ivy bush

897 – Halfback (football)

898 – half-paved

899 – Half bib

900 – Buses, bosses

901 – Pastor

902 – Bison

903 – Pacemaker

904 – Pacer

905 – Pussy willow

906 – Pasture

907 – Bicycle

908 – Pacifier

909 – Baseball

910 – Beads

911 – Potato

912 – Baton

913 – Badminton

914 – Battery

915 – Pedal

916 – Beautician

917 – Bodyguard

918 – Boat Full

919 – Bat boy,

920 – Pencil

921 – Bayonet

922 – Banana

923 – Panama (Canal or hat)

924 – Pioneer

925 – Panel

926 – Pawnshop, poncho, Banjo

927 – Pancake, pin cushion, Bank

928 – Pinfish, bonfire, Bowie Knife

929 – Pinball

930 – Beams

931 – Beamed (ceiling)

932 – Pimento

933 – Boom man (crane Operator)

934 – Boomerang

935 – Palm oil

936 – Bombshell

937 – Pomegranate

938 – Pamphlet

939 – Bambi

940 – Purse

941 – Pirate

942 – Piranha

943 – Barmaid

944 – Prayer

945 – Pearl

946 – Brush

947 – Brick

948 – Perfume

949 – Barbecue

950 – Pills

951 – Bullet

952 – Balloon

953 – Palomino

954 – Polar (bear)

955 – Pool hall

956 – Blue Jay

957 – Pelican

958 – Billfold

959 – Pallbearer

960 – Badges,

961 – Poached (Eggs)

962 – Pageant

963 – Pajamas

964 – Pusher (drugs)

965 – Pugilist

966 – Beach shoe (sandals)

967 – Paycheck

968 – Pitchfork

969 – Bishop

970 – Pigskin

971 – Picket

972 – Bacon

973 – Pac-Man

974 – Packer

975 – Pickle

976 – Bookshelf

977 – Peacock

978 – pick-off (baseball)

979 – Bagpipe

980 – Beehives

981 – Beef tongue

982 – Bouffant (hair style)

983 – Pavement

984 – Beaver

985 – Buffalo

986 –Beef Jerky

987 – Bifocals

988 – Beef feeder

989 – Beef burger

990 – Bobsled

991 – Puppet

992 – Baboon

993 – Pipe man

994 – Pepper

995 – Bible

996 – pea patch

997 – Popcorn

998 – baby face

999 – Baby bib

1,000 – Diseases

This list is more for reference. I have been teaching memory seminars for 2 decades now, and I am one of only a handful of people that I know of who has memorized this list. If you chose to do so, good for you! On the other hand, pictures for numbers 1-100 will be great for most applications.

Memorizing the Presidents

Welcome back to Day 18. How are you? Are you memorizing a 100-digit number yet? Well, probably not right now, but I'm sure you are well on your way. Remember, you will just need 50 files to accomplish this feat. We are going to spend the next few days working on names and faces. Names and faces are probably one of the most rewarding aspects of memory training. Dale Carnegie's book, *How To Win Friends And Influence People* is one of the best-selling books of all time. In that book, Dale Carnegie discovered two important facts; one is that everyone's favorite subject is actually him or her self; the second is that the sweetest sound to a person's ear, universally, in any language, is the sound of their own name.

Now, be honest with me. Knowing that everybody's favorite subject is themselves, and the sweetest sound to the ear is a person's own name, how many times have you been introduced to someone and as soon as that handshake breaks, boom, the name drops to the floor? It is very embarrassing, but it happens to all of us. When you recall someone's name, you have just set yourself apart from the rest of the group in their mind. You have made a distinction between you and the others. The next question is, "Well great, Ronnie, but how do you do it?" Good question, I'm glad that you asked.

What are the 5 things that we need to recall anything? Focus, Location, Code, Action and Review. We utilize this knowledge to recall names also. People's faces are actually the file. The code we use is the picture, and that picture is determined by the name.

We are going to have a memory test, and this actually will help us with name memory. Your goal is to memorize this list of words below. Don't spend more than 10 minutes memorizing it, and see if you can memorize it faster than that. There are 44 words, so you decide BEFORE you start which 44 files you are going to use.

1. Washing Machine

2. A Dam

3. Chef cooking the sun

4. Medicine

5. Man in a row boat

6. A Dam and Cue Balls

7. Car jack

8. Van on fire

9. Hair

10. Tie

11. Polka dots

12. Tailor

13. Filling up a glass

14. Earring

15. Blue Cannon

16. Beard

17. Ants drawing

18. College Campus

19. Fog, Mist or Haze

20. Garfield the cat

21. Author

22. City of Cleveland

23. Benji, the Walt Disney Dog

24. City of Cleveland

25. Mount McKinley (in Alaska)

26. Roses

27. Raft

28. Wilson tennis ball

29. Hard surface

30. Cooler

31. Vacuum cleaner

32. Roses

33. Man telling truth

34. Eyeball

35. Ken doll (Barbie and Barbie)

36. Airplane 'landing'

37. Gate with water rushing through it

38. Ford truck

39. Peanut Butter

40. Jelly Beans

41. Bushes

42. Lint

43. Bushes

44. Bahamas

There you have it. Now number 1-44 and see how many words that you recall. Remember the answer doesn't come to mind right away skip it and continue. Don't get slowed down with the ones that you don't recall. Finish the ones that you do know and then return to the ones that you initially missed.

So what do you think we just memorized? Well, we were talking about names so if you guessed 44 names then you are correct! But let's take it one step further, these are important names! They are the names of the 44 Presidents of The United States! Many students will spend days or weeks memorizing the presidents of the United States and you did it in only MINUTES!

Here are the answers:

1. Washing Machine = Washington

2. A Dam = Adams

3. Chef cooking the sun = Jefferson (Chef Sun)

4. Medicine = Madison

5. Man in a row boat = Monroe

6. A Dam and Cue Balls = Q. Adams

7. Car jack = Jackson

8. Van on fire = Van Buren (Van burning)

9. Hair = Harrison

10. Tie = Tyler

11. Polka dots = Polk

12. Tailor = Taylor

13. Filling up a glass more = Fillmore

14. Ear ring = Pierce (ear pierced to get an ear ring)

15. Blue Cannon = Buchanan

16. Beard = Abe Lincoln

17. Ants drawing = Andrew (Johnson)

18. College Campus = Grant (college grant)

19. Fog, mist or Haze = Hayes

20. Garfield the cat = Garfield

21. Author = Arthur

22. City of Cleveland = Cleveland

23. Benji – the Walt Disney Dog = Benjamin (Harrison)

24. City of Cleveland = Cleveland

25. Mount McKinley (in Alaska) = McKinley

26. Roses = Roosevelt

27. Raft = Taft

28. Wilson tennis ball = Wilson

29. Hard surface = Harding

30. Cooler = Coolidge

31. Vacuum cleaner = Hoover

32. Roses = Franklin Roosevelt

33. Man telling truth = Truman

34. Eyeball = Eisenhower

35. Ken doll (Barbie and Barbie) = Kennedy

36. Airplane 'landing' = Lyndon (landing) Johnson

37. Gate with water rushing through it = Nixon (Water Gate)

38. Ford truck = Ford

39. Peanut Butter = Jimmy Carter (His family was in the peanut business)

40. Jelly Beans = Reagan (his favorite candy)

41. Bushes = Bush

42. Lint = Clinton

43. Bushes = Bush

44. Bahamas = Obama

There you have it! The 44 presidents!

Now, let's go back to names and faces. The five things that you need to recall a name are: focus, location, a code, action and review. All we are going to focus on today is the code, or turning names into pictures. We will concentrate on the others tomorrow and the next day. So, knowing that every name must be a picture to recall it, let's see what we have. Just to let you know, yes, everyone I meet I have a picture for his or her name. I met a gentleman today, he said, "Ronnie, I never forget a face, but I'm terrible with names." The reason for that is you see the face but you don't see the name. It is abstract to you. In order to recall a name, you have to see it, just like you saw the face.

How many times have you been out and you see someone you know but you don't know where you know them from? Then they walk up to you and they say, "Hey, Ronnie, how are you?" And you say, "Good!" and you wish you could recall their name, and then two hours later, when you're driving home, the name pops up in your head. What does that prove? Well, actually it proves a couple of things. Number one, we recall faces better than names because we see the face and not the name. The second thing that it teaches us is that our mind never actually forgets a name. Accessing and retrieving the name is the difficulty. The name is up there, but getting to it when we need it is the problem. So, let's use this knowledge to our benefit.

Now, at this point, people always say to me, "Wait a minute, Ronnie. Are you telling me that every time I meet someone, I'm going to have to go through this whole process and turn their name into a picture?" My answer to that is, "No." Then they get a confused look on their face. The first time that you meet someone, the first time you meet a Ronnie, a Michelle, an Eric, an Allen, or a Debbie, you'll have to turn the name into a picture. However, the next time you meet Ronnie, Michelle, Eric, or Allen, the work is already done. You will have the picture already made. You have already done it, because you did it the first time. So, in review of today's lesson, let's focus on what we just did. We took 44 names and turned them into pictures. Today, when I meet people, I am not turning their names into pictures. For the most part, I already have the names. I'm just sticking their names on the locations or files that I have established.

Names and Faces

Hey, it's Day 19! Are you ready to advance to the next level of names memory? At this point, you understand that to recall someone's name, you have to see their name just as you see their face. Your mind remembers pictures. Have you heard the saying that a picture is worth a thousand words? In this case it is just worth one word. But that word is the sweetest sound to a person's ear.

Now that we have worked on turning names into pictures, let's focus on where we are going to store the code, or where we are going to store the person's name. The location, of course, is the person's face. When you meet someone, whether you are doing this consciously or subconsciously, you are doing that. When you meet someone you look at their face and you notice certain features. For example, if you met Jay Leno, you would notice an outstanding facial feature. What would it be? Perhaps the chin. What about David Letterman? Maybe the gap in his teeth. What about Telly Savalas? Well, his head is bald. If you meet Abraham Lincoln, his beard would be his outstanding feature. Most everyone has something on their face that draws your attention. Even the most beautiful person has beautiful eyes that draw your attention, or perhaps their lips, or mouth, or nose or eyebrows.

Next you will see 15 faces and on each one of these faces, we are going to choose an outstanding feature.

Let's look at number one face together. We will pretend that we are meeting this individual for the first time. The outstanding feature we are going to choose on this face is the bushy eyebrows. So, picture number one as Mr. Eyebrows. Now, don't write the name in the guidebook just yet. We are going to do that later. Just concentrate on the faces for now. Say hello to Mr. Eyebrows.

Now, on to face number two. On this lady's face, make the file her cheekbones. Say hello to Miss Cheekbones. Go back and review Mr. Eyebrows, now say hello to Miss Cheekbones. Number 3, let's call this gentleman Mr. Beard, because he has a beard and that is our file. Look at him and say, "Hello, Mr. Beard." Face number 4, let's call this face Miss Eyes because of her large eyes. Number 4 is Miss Eyes because of her large eyes. Say hello to Miss Eyes. Number 5 the feature is his mustache. Number 5 is Mr. Mustache. Go back and review one through 5. What was one, number two, number 3, number 4 and 5?

Now we are on number 6. Let's call this guy Mr. Forehead, because of his high forehead. Number 7 has large ears, so number 7 is Mr. Ears because of his large ears. Real quick, go back and review number 6, number 5, number 4, number 3, number two, and one. Now we are on number 8. Let's make number eight Miss Lips because of her full lips. Number 8 is Miss Lips because of her full lips. Look at number 4. What was this person's name? Number 9, what do you think we will call this person? How about Miss Mole for the mole on her face. Miss mole is our ninth face. Here, we are on number 10. Look at this face. Let's call this face Mr. Glasses because of his glasses. Now, it is important not to use sunglasses or reading glasses because they may not have them on the next time you see them. However, if they look to be permanent, and glasses are terrific, they definitely distinguish a face. Remember and review the ones before. Look at face number one. Look at face number two, number 3, number 4 and number 5.

How about number 6, number 7, number 8, number 9 and 10? Ok, let's look at the next face and let's call this face Mr. Scar for the scar on his cheek. Mr. Scar. Say hello to Mr. Scar. Number 12, look at the face and call her Miss Teeth. Look at her pretty teeth and smile. Number 13, let's call this face Mr. Wrinkle for the wrinkles on his face. Number 14, call this face Mr. Dimple for the dimple on his chin. Dimples on the chin are safe to use. Sometimes dimples on a face can only be seen when a person smiles, and those are dangerous because they may not be smiling when you see them the next time. The last one, number 15, let's call this face Mr. Nose for his large nose. Mr. Nose is number 15. Look back quickly and review the ones before. What we are going to do right now is going to go back and write the names we have just given the people in the space provided below their picture. So write the names.

How did you do? Did you get all the new names? I think that you will find this pretty successful. Now you say, "Sure, Ronnie, I was able to do that, but the problem is that this is not the person's real name." You're right, if you can do this, then you are not going to have any problem recalling their name. So far, you understand to recall a person's name, you must turn their name into a picture, which is actually what we covered yesterday. The second thing you need to do is observe the face, and pick a distinguishing feature. These two ingredients are going to work in tandem when you recall a name. We will work tomorrow on how to put these two items together, but do not move to Day 20 unless you understand everything we have talked about today. So, we have come to a conclusion here on Day 19.

Names and Faces

The ability to recall a person's name will light up their eyes. It makes people feel important! I can't tell you how many times I've been tapped on the shoulder in line for a movie in Dallas and someone will say, "Ok, Mr. Memory, what's my name now?" About 70% of the time I can recall their name. What's more important, about 70% of the time, they will recall my name. Why? I'm nothing different or special over anyone else. The only thing that I did when I left was to call them by their names. That is what differentiated me in their mind. It obligates people to recall you when you recall them.

We have already established the location is the person's face, and that is why we chose a facial feature. The next thing that we established was that the code was the name turned into a picture. And now, we're up to the next step- the action where we put the two together. Do you recall on Day 18 when we turned names into pictures and then filed them to our house files? Recalling a name works the same way, except that the difference is that instead of filing the name to a piece of furniture, we're filing it to a face. There is absolutely no difference.

Looking at these faces we are now going to memorize the names with the face:

I'm going to give you two pictures to file to each person's face. Take these pictures and then file them to the entire face, but remember the action should be centered around or focused on the person's outstanding feature – that was the purpose of picking it out. Let's look at the face for number one. Now, do not write anything down until you are instructed to do so. Remember this is a memory program. Here we go! This person's name is John Webster. First turn his name into a picture. The picture for

John is a toilet and Webster is from Webster's Dictionary. Looking at a picture, first we are going to file a toilet and a dictionary to his eyebrows. This is just like what we did to our house files, but the only difference is that we filed it to someone's face.

Now, let's move on to the second face. This person's name is Debbie Wayne. The picture for Debbie is dead bee and the picture for Wayne is rain. Every time you meet a Debbie, the picture is a dead bee, and the picture for Wayne is always rain. Now, let's focus on her facial file. We see that it was her cheekbones. As you look at her picture, begin to notice that there is a dead bee on each of her cheekbones and is being showered by rain. Perhaps you just met this woman in a social situation and you see this dead bee and rain on her face. Remember to focus the action around her cheekbones. The next time you see her cheekbones, that will be the brain trigger. Review number one. What was his name? John Webster. Review the picture. What was number 2's name? Debbie Wayne.

Number 3. This gentleman's name is Paul Russ. Every Paul is a basketball and every Russ is rust. As we decided yesterday, our file for this gentleman is his beard. So, as you look at this man's face, visualize yourself dribbling a basketball made out of rust on his beard. Again, look at the beard, and visualize a basketball made out of rust being dribbled on his beard. Use all your senses. Imagine the taste and smell, and feel the basketball made out of rust. His name is Paul Russ.

Number 4. This lady's name is Ann Green. The picture for Ann is "ants," and the picture for green is "green"! The file for this woman is her eyes, so we are going to file ants in her eyes and they are all green. Now, remember that your pictures for these things need to be larger than life. Make the ants huge, and they are crawling around in her eyes and they're green. Maybe they're crawling out of her eyes, and they come out and are coming to get you. Now, that would be somewhat of a gross picture, but guess what, you won't soon forget it. So file ants and green to your file, and it's Ann Green. Review the ones before.

Number 5. What is your file? That's right, your file is the mustache. This gentleman's file is a mustache, and his name is Chris Gordon. The picture for Chris is a cross, and the picture for Gordon is a garden. So look at this man. You notice that his mustache is really a garden and it is growing nothing but crosses! That is a picture! A garden that is growing nothing but crosses. Again, his name is Chris Gordon. Cross for Chris and garden for Gordon.

Number 6, his file is the high forehead. His name is Mark Reeves. Every Mark is a marker, like the one you write with, and Reeves is a reef, like the Great Barrier Reef or a coral reef. On this gentleman's forehead, visualize a marker drawing a reef on his forehead. Again, draw a coral reef on this gentleman's head with a marker. This gentleman's name is Mark Reeves. Mark Reeves. Look at his picture and visualize the image that we just described.

Number 7. What was the file? It was ears. This gentleman's name is Steve Light. Every Steve is a stove and every Light is a light bulb. We said that his ears are the file, so we are going to put his large ears in the stove. We are cooking his ears and then the light bulb goes off and tells us that the cooking is done. Remember, don't just say it – see it! Saying it does little, but seeing it does everything.

Number 8, what is the file? The file for this one is full lips. The lady's name is Margaret and her last name is Sanders. The picture for Margaret is a margarita and the picture for Sanders is a sander. As you observe this woman's face, you notice she is drinking a margarita that is nothing but sand. Perhaps the sand is all over her lips and her teeth, and she smiles as she drinks the sand margarita.

Number 9. This lady's name is Elizabeth Smith. The picture for Elizabeth is a lizard with bad breath, and the picture for Smith is always a blacksmith iron. As you look at the picture of this lady, a lizard with really bad breath comes to sit on her mole. You, not liking lizards, decide to kill it with a blacksmith's iron. So, look at her picture and see yourself branding this lizard with a blacksmith's branding iron.

Number 10. We have decided that on his face the file was going to be his glasses, right? His name is Al Cash. Every Al is an owl, and Cash is, of course, money. The pictures that we are going to put on his face are an owl and money. Look at this picture and see an owl in his glasses, and the owl is made out of money. Every time he opens his mouth to hoot, a quarter comes out! Look at the picture and visualize this taking place on his glasses. Now, owl is for the name, Al. And money is for the last name, Cash. Say hello to Al Cash. Go back and review the ones from before. See the picture and then recall what the name stood for. Number one, number two, 3, 4, 5, 6, 7, 8, 9, and 10, review them all.

This is how you memorize names. Go back now and see how many of the names that you can recall.

So, how did you do? Did you get all of them? I bet you did pretty well. If you were able to see these pictures then it wasn't difficult at all. If you didn't see the picture, then that was a challenge. If you were able to recall the picture but not the name, don't worry. These pictures were mine. In real life, you will be creating the pictures that will be representing the names, so you are not going to have a problem recalling what the picture stood for. It will be obvious to you because it was your picture.

Let's grade your test real quick before we wrap it up for today. Number one was John Webster. Number two was Debbie Wayne. Three was Paul Russ. Four is Ann Green. Five is Chris Gordon. Six is Mark Reeves. Seven is Steve Light. Eight is Margaret Sanders. Nine is Elizabeth Smith. And 10 was, of course, Al Cash. There you have it. Ten names, 10 pictures, and 10 faces.

In real life it's no different than this process. Always repeat the person's name in the conversation. When I'm going home after a meeting with someone, I'll review their name in their facial files, and then I will even review it a few days later. Is it a little bit of work? You'd better believe it is! However, is it worth it? When you see a person 6 months after you have met them and you recall their name, then you have just placed yourself in a very select category. You have made them feel good about themselves, and you have just gone from the level of acquaintance to friend. And, believe me, it's worth every ounce of effort, so keep this in mind. When I'm meeting people today, I don't have to ask myself, "What is the picture for this person's name?" You already are going to have the pictures for every Robert. Once you do it, it's done. For every Lisa, you do it once. For every John, once, and so on. Initially, this system will take a little bit of work to build up the encyclopedia of names, however, once your encyclopedia of names is built up, this is as easy as 1, 2, 3.

The challenge that I lay down for you is this – every time you meet a person over the next three to four weeks, turn their name into a picture. If you are at the movie theatre, bank, ATM machine, grocery store, church, school, gas station or at an office, turn the name of the person that you meet into a picture. When you meet a Steve, ask yourself, "What is a picture for Steve?" Once you determine what it is, then use that picture for every Steve. My picture for Steve is a stove. So EVERYTIME I meet a Steve I see a stove. Do not, and I repeat – DO NOT, use the picture of a stove one day, and the next time you meet a Steve create a different picture for Steve. This will only complicate the process.

Here are a few examples:

Karen = Carrot	David = Divot
Michelle = Missle	Tom = Tomcat
Wendi = Wind	Abby = A bee
Kyle = Tile	Paul = Ball
Hilary = Hill of Trees	Crystal = Crystal
Lisa = Mona Lisa	Nancy = Nun eating seeds
Rick = Brick	Candy = Candy
Don = Sunrise	Dan = Pan
Dave = Cave	Linda = Window

Names and Faces

The key to remembering when meeting someone is to focus on their face and distinguishing features. Then take their name and turn it into a picture, and with action tie that picture to the face. We are going to go through the same drill as we did on Day 20. This time, we are just going to meet 5 people. Actually, you have already met these people before. They are left over from Day 19. You have their outstanding facial features, now you just need their names. Remember that their whole face is actually where you store the name. The outstanding facial feature is where you put the picture on where it's focused.

This is Miss Teeth, remember her? Her name is Judy Rose. The picture for Judy is chewing tea and the picture for Rose is a rose. So, look at the picture and at her teeth. The picture is her chewing tea bags for Judy. Remember to incorporate all your senses. See it, hear it, taste it. You have chewing tea for Judy, now maybe a rose in her hair or in her mouth. After she chews the tea, she chews the rose to get the taste out of her mouth.

Number two. This is Mr. Scar. His name is Brian Nichols. The picture for Brian is a brain and the picture for Nichols is nickels – money, like the nickels you spend. So, let's look at the picture, and specifically the scar. Act as if this is a real person you are meeting for the first time. As you are looking at the scar, you see a brain poking out of the scar. You grab some nickels and you cover up the exposed brain. Wow! You're covering up his exposed brain with nickels!

The next face is Mr. Wrinkle. His name is Dan Frog. Every Dan is a pan, like a pan you cook with and, of course, Frog is a frog. Look at Mr. Wrinkle and on his face is a pan and cooking in the pan is a frog. His face is actually a stove that is cooking frogs. As you are talking to him, maybe you reach down in the pan and you decide to have some frog legs.

The next one is Mr. Dimple because of the dimple in his chin. His name is Craig Robbins. Every Craig is a keg, and every Robbins is the bird – a robin. Let's look at this gentleman, and resting on his chin is a keg, and several robins have gathered around and are drinking out of the keg. This gentleman is actually a walking bird feeder. Every time you see him, he has a swarm of robins around him feeding off the keg on his chin; you'd never forget it, and tell everybody about it!

The last gentleman is Mr. Nose. His name is Tom Lewis. Every Tom is a tomcat, and every Lewis is a loose "s." Moving all around the gentleman's nose is a loose "s." It's running around like crazy! Can you guess what's chasing the "s"? Sure, I bet you can, a cat – a tomcat to be precise.

This should be getting a little bit clearer and easier. I hope that you are following along just fine. Is this the process that you will be going through whenever you meet a person? The answer to that question is – absolutely yes. Don't let that discourage you. This is an aspect of memory training that requires a little bit of effort. However, if it didn't require effort, it wouldn't be worth it. Also, remember that the effort is at the beginning. The work is going to be building up an encyclopedia of names. The first time ever that I spoke to a company as a memory-training speaker I only called on three people because I only wanted to be responsible to retain three names. As I got more confident in the system, I slowly worked my way up. Today, it is no big deal for me to meet fifty people in thirty minutes and recall their names. However, I did not start there, and you will not either. Don't get discouraged because you can't recall 5 people right now. You are going to meet people today and tomorrow anyway, so turn their name into a picture. Just give it a try. I think you'll be impressed, and remember – I review the name on the way home after I meet someone and even a few days later. You have to if you want to cement it in.

Fun Memory Demonstrations

Today is going to be a fun day. I'm going to teach you some memory games or stunts you can play with your friends. These are neat demonstrations of a trained memory. There are several purposes that these games have. Number one, you get to have some fun. Number two, you get to practice the system. Number 3, people will get to ask you how you did it! You will get the privilege of teaching them the system.

The first demonstration is actually one I saw a memory expert show on the *Tonight Show* with Johnny Carson. It got quite a reaction, and it was actually very simple. The memory expert used 50 files. Johnny handed him a magazine, and gave him a few minutes to look at it while Johnny went on with the show. When they came back to the memory expert, Johnny took the magazine back and said, "What did page 23 talk about?" The expert said, "The article was talking about motorcycles." Everyone applauded. He said, "Ok, Mr. Bigshot, what about page 47?" He said, "That was the ad about the trip to Hawaii." This blew everyone away. However, with a little bit of understanding in memory training we could figure out what he was doing. He glanced at every page, got the general idea, turned it into a picture, then filed that to his file. He did this with 50 files and that was pretty easy, actually. However, it got quite a reaction, and it should get a reaction if you do it as a demonstration. That is a fun one.

Another fun memory stunt is to memorize the serial numbers on dollar bills. Have everyone hand you a dollar bill. To do this, you must understand phonics and have pictures for two digit numbers. Look at the serial numbers, and then file them to your house files. You must also turn the letters into pictures. A is ax, b is a bicycle, c is a computer, d is a drum and so on. You have 5 rooms in your files. Make each room dedicated to a bill. File the pictures to your files and you should amaze everyone. Don't bet money when you do these stunts, your friends probably won't be your friends for long if you take money from them.

Here's another neat stunt. Write out 50 to 100 numbers on a sheet of paper. Give the paper to a friend and have him circle 5 numbers. Then, tell him to call out all the numbers that he has on his paper except the ones he circled. Tell him to do this in random order. As he is doing this, you are mutilating the file he is calling out. Maybe you are destroying it, or throwing water on it, or setting it on fire. It really doesn't matter what you do, just change it up somehow. When he gets done going through your files, the 5 that you have done nothing to are the ones that he circled. This makes the hair stand up on the back of people's neck. Quite a feat!

Here's another fun one. Have you ever wanted to learn the calendar for an entire year? Well, it's actually easier than you think. It is going to take just 12 files and each file represents a month of the year. For example, January is represented by a baby. February is represented by Cupid. March is soldiers marching. April is an umbrella. May is flowers. June is a June bug. July is fire crackers. August is the sun. September is a school. October is a pumpkin. November is a turkey. And December is a Christmas tree. The next item of business is to determine the first Sunday of every month. For example, if the first Sunday in January is the fifth, you will file a star to baby. You use the pencil list and the picture from their file to your 12-month files. Then when someone asks you, "What day of the week is the 23rd of January?" You say, well, that's a Thursday. All you have to do is count from the first Sunday by 7s until you get to the week that the day in question falls on. If it is one number away, you know it is Monday. Two days away, it is Tuesday, 3 days away it is Wednesday, 4 is Thursday, 5 is Friday and 6 is Saturday. All you have to do is learn the first Sunday of all 12 months and you have a neat little demonstration that you can do. This one is more than just a memory stunt. You will actually be able to use this to help you in your life.

When you're sitting in a board meeting and someone says, "Let's meet again on the 18th of June," you can say, "That is no good because that's a Sunday." Everyone asks, "Did he memorize the whole calendar?" No. But you never pass up an opportunity to demonstrate the system.

Other memory games can be just as fun. Have someone give you items and file them to your files. People love this! I encourage you to teach the system after you do this demo. Don't hog the spotlight. People will appreciate your willingness to share. These are just some of the games, there are many more. If you think of some on your own, send me a letter or email. I always like to have fun with this system.

Memorizing a Deck of Cards

This is one of my favorite memory demonstrations! I love to get a deck of cards and shuffle them up, and then race through them in a little over a minute, then hand the deck to someone and I will call off the cards in order as they flip them over! POWERFUL and FUN!

There are many systems out there to memorize a deck of cards, but the one I am going to describe below is incredibly powerful and is used by memory experts all over the world to memorize a deck of cards in under 27 seconds! Yes, you read that right! Ben Pridmore of the United Kingdom has memorized a deck of cards in 26.2 seconds! Dominic O'Brien has memorized 54 decks (2808 cards) and David Farrow 59 decks (3068)! There systems may not be exactly like the one I will describe below but it is pretty close.

When I memorize a deck of cards I am memorizing 3 cards at a time. Remember earlier when we talked about character/action/object for numbers. Well, I also have character/action/object for every card. There are many ways that you can do this. Personally this is how I have done it.

I assigned a number to every card:

The numbers 2 to 14 represents spades. The 2 of spades represents the number 2 in my mind. The 10 of spades represents the number 10 in my mind. Jack = 11, Queen = 12, King = 13 and Ace = 14

Hearts are represented by the numbers 22 to 34. The 2 of hearts is the number 22 in my mind. The 10 of hearts represents the number 30. Jack = 31, Queen = 32, King = 33 and Ace = 34

Diamonds are represented by the numbers 42 to 54. The 2 of diamonds is the same as the number 42 in my mind. The 10 of diamonds represents the number 50. Jack = 51, Queen = 52, King = 53 and Ace = 54.

Clubs are represented by the numbers 60 to 74 in my mind. The 2 of clubs represents the number 62. The 10 of clubs represents the number 70. Jack = 71, Queen = 72, King = 73 and Ace = 74

The next step is to think of a person that goes with each number. 33 could be your mom because using the phonics we discovered before 3 is "muh," 33 = mom. What does your mom like to do? Maybe cook? So the action would be cooking and the object would be a frying pan. The character/action/object for you would be mom cooking in a pan. This all represents the number 33 for you, and more importantly, the King of Hearts.

You can create the characters (people) this way using numbers and phonics. I like this method because it kills two birds with one stone. You are also creating pictures for numbers this way! You can create your own rules. I have a friend named Kristen Payne and she represents the number 79 for me because 79 is 'Kuh' and 'Puh'. Thus we have the initials K.P. But I don't always use the initials, my picture for 65 is a friend of mine named Ashley. Because 6 is 'shuh' and 5 is 'luh'. So the number 65 is "Ashley" for me. You are going to have to develop your own method.

Another way to create the character/action/object is you could create pictures based on something like this:

- Every card in the hearts suit is someone that you love.

- Every card in the club suit is someone that is famous.

- Every card in the spades suit is someone you work with.

- Every card in the diamond suit is someone rich.

Then after you have created the person/character for each card, then you create an action and object that would go with that card. For example if Albert Einstein becomes one of your characters then your action might be experimenting and the object might be a test tube.

Now, hopefully this makes sense and you are able to create a character/action/object for each card.

Then you start memorizing!

You take the first 3 cards and they are: the King of Hearts, Ace of Spades and Jack of Diamonds. You create a quick story using the character for the first card, the action for the second card and the object for the third card. You then file this to your first file. You do this with 17 files, and then on the 18th file you just put one character. After you have done this, you mentally go back through your files, and on each file you should have a character/action/object. The character is the first card, the action is the second card and the object is the third card.

There you have it! You now know how the memory experts memorize a deck of cards in less than a minute. Practice this method until you get really good, and then I hope to see you at a championship soon!

Memorizing Scripture

Do you recall the pencil list? Let's review it together. Number one is a pencil because it looks like a number one. Number two is a sink because it has two options, on and off. Number 3 is a ring for a 3-ring circus. Number 4 is a track – 4 times around is a mile. Number 5 is a star because it has 5 points. Number 6 is a bullet, a 6-shooter, or 6 feet under. Number 7 is dice, lucky 7, opposite sides always equal 7. Number 8 is an hourglass shaped like an 8. Number 9 is a baseball – 9 players, 9 innings. Number 10 is fingers – 10 fingers, 10 toes.

Number 11 is a goal post – 11 players on a team, a goal post is shaped like an 11. Number 12 is eggs – a dozen eggs. Number 13 is the flag – representing 13 stars, 13 stripes, or 13 original colonies. Number 14, what was that? A necklace is 14 karat gold – 14 of Valentine's Day (February 14). How about 15, remember that one? It was paycheck, the first and the 15th is when you get paid. Number 16, what was it? You got car, right? At sixteen you get your driver's license. Number 17, what is it? *Seventeen* Magazine. There's a magazine called *Seventeen*. Number 18, what was it? A soldier, remember at 18 you register for the draft? Number 19, what was that? Golf clubs, you better believe it. The 19th hole. And number 20 is a shotgun. Why? a Twenty-gauge shotgun. Using basic association created this list. It is also a filing system because there is more than one item, and they are filed in a logical order.

There are 20 files. It also demonstrates to us what basic association is. This is a list that could be used to file anything, and remember that whatever you want to recall you have to turn into a picture. That is the code, the hard drive that your mind thinks with. If you want to recall lines of poetry or a quote, remember all you have to do is get a general idea and turn it into a picture, and then file that file to your pencil list.

There are 20 files that had unlimited possibilities. Now we may have another file system that we want to keep fresh in your minds, and that is our skeleton files. This is a 10-file filing system, and works great for a lot of different possibilities.

I taught a seminar in New Orleans last year. Before it was my turn to speak the company offered $50 to anyone who could say the mission statement. One gentleman out of the whole company could say it. I stood up and said, "How many of you think I could teach you the mission statement forwards, backwards, in and out of order, or by number in less than 7 minutes?" No one believed me. However, they were all eager with anticipation. Everyone wanted to be able to do it. We broke their mission statement down into 10 lines, and we turned each one of those lines into a picture, and then simply filed those to our skeleton files. In just a few short minutes we had memorized their company's mission statement. Everyone was amazed.

I bring up this story for this reason. Perhaps there are times when you are memorizing information using this system that you may be thinking to yourself, "This is no big deal. This isn't that hard." If that is what you are thinking, then you're right. It isn't hard because we are approaching it from the correct angle the first time. If we were using rote memorization first, and then learned this system – as the company in New Orleans, you would see the difference. Keep in mind that when someone gives me a list of 15 to 25 words, and I memorize it forwards and backwards, and by number, it blows them away. You have seen that demo, and that is most likely why you taking this program. If that is true, remember this, you were impressed with the results, not the process. Just because you know the process, do not let that change the fact that this is a very impressive demonstration.

Now, let's review our skeleton files. They are number one, on top;

two is nose; 3 is mouth; 4 is ribs; 5 is liver; 6 is joint; 7 is cap; 8 is fibula; 9 is ball; and 10 is sand. Now, these are our files. I recently did a program in Norfolk, Virginia where I was asked to teach a group the Ten Commandments, and they wanted to know them forwards and backwards, and by number. I taught them the skeleton files and then we learned the Ten Commandments using the skeleton files.

Let's do this together. What is your file? It is top. The First Commandment is to have no other gods. We must turn that phrase into a picture. Make a picture in your mind of what having no other gods before represents to you. For some people it may be money, power, fame, or something that they put as the ultimate in their life that represents their god. When you hear the verse, have no other gods before me, file that picture to your top.

Number two, what is your file? It is nose. The Second Commandment says you shall not make a graven image. Let's focus on two words, graven and image and file a tombstone to your nose. Do you see the correlation? Tombstone marks a grave? Touch your nose right now with your finger and imagine a tombstone crushing your finger and your nose.

Number 3 is your mouth, and the Third Commandment states: "Do not take the name of the Lord in vain." Your file is mouth. Open your mouth really wide and imagine you are writing your name all over your teeth with a marker. Every time you smile you will have your name written all over your teeth. For example, my teeth say Ronnie all over them.

Now, what is your number 4 file? It's your ribs. The Fourth Commandment is to keep the Sabbath holy. The substitute picture for Sabbath is a bath. Sabbath is a bath. File your ribs getting a bath.

The next file is your liver. The Fifth Commandment is, honor your father and mother. Close your eyes and see a picture of your mother and father in your mind. Now take that picture and with action, file it to your liver. Maybe you see your mom and your dad standing on your liver, or they are on the inside trying to get out.

Number 6, what is your file? It is your joint. The Sixth Commandment states you shall not murder. Have someone sticking a knife into your hip joint. This is the verse, thou shall not murder.

Number 7, what is your file? It's your cap, right? The Seventh Commandment is: thou shall not commit adultery. File a tree growing out of your kneecap, and a doll is hanging on the tree. A doll on a tree, adultery.

Number 8, what is your file? It is the fibula. The Eighth Commandment is that you shall not steal. What do you think of when I say steal? Is it the act of stealing something, or a steel bar, or is it Superman because he's the man of steel. For the purposes of this, let's use Superman. Look down at your fibula, and Superman lands there and is standing on your leg. You reach down and pat him on the head. You tell everyone, "Hey, look! It's the man of steel!

Number 9, what is it? It is a ball, as in the ball of your foot. This commandment says you do not bear false witness. So, let's just get a brain trigger for false. Let's file a red light bulb for false. Can you see a red light bulb and it's flashing, perhaps the light breaks and cuts your foot?

Number 10 is sand. I want you to file a Corvette. What color do you like the best? Does it have leather seats? See it so you won't forget it. File it to sand. What does a Corvette have to do with the Tenth Commandment? Number 10 says, thou shalt not covet. Covet is an abstract, but you can see Corvette. So, number 10 is thou shall not covet.

Review and see how many that you recall.

How did you do? Did you get all 10? If you didn't get a perfect score, remember, and I've said this a million times, it is but of two reasons: Either didn't know your file; or your action wasn't vivid enough. Most the time you will not recall an item because it is not vivid enough. That is the key to this whole system. Let's go through them one through 10 and see how you did.

1. Something that you worship

2. Grave

3. Writing a name

4. Taking a bath

5. Mother and father

6. Knife

7. Doll in a tree

8. Superman

9. Light bulb

10. Corvette

Now, if you're saying, "Ronnie, this is good because I can remember the picture, but I'm having a hard time recalling what these items stood for." That is not a problem, not at all. The reason for that is because these are my pictures, and this information is just for practice. If this was information that was important to you, and you were turning the abstracts into pictures, then you would know what the pictures stood for when the time comes. Practice these techniques with your friends. Have them give you 15 or 20, or even 30 or 50 items. File them to your files, and encourage your friend to give them to you quickly. However, speed is not the main concern in this situation. The main concern is making sure that you understand the concepts.

Working on Speed Memory

If there is one thing that I have done that has impacted my memory more than anything in the last year it is that I have pushed my mind on the issue of speed. As I type this, just 10 short months ago it took me over 6 minutes to memorize a deck of 52 shuffled cards! About two months ago I was down to 3 minutes! I was excited and I emailed my memory coach (yes I have a memory coach!). His name is David Thomas. He is a man who has held a Guinness World Record by memorizing pi to over 20,000 digits and has won the USA Memory Championship (2007). He placed very well at the World Memory Championship level (which is VERY hard to do). At any rate, I emailed him and shared my excitement at being able to memorize a deck of cards in 3 minutes. He commended my speed, but then urged me to be able to do it in 2 minutes! I thought, "Wow! He doesn't understand how I never thought I would get to 3 minutes!" However, I pressed on.

Ben Pridmore, who is the current record holder for memorizing a deck of cards in 26.2 seconds, gave me similar advice. He said, "Don't wait until you are 100% sure that the image is in your memory. Instead, move to the next file and keep going. You will be surprised when you return to the file to discover that information is still in your memory."

Ben's philosophy was to move rapidly, and trust your memory that is will store the data at a higher rate of speed.

Both Ben and David were correct. It took me 8 months to go from 6 minutes to 3 minutes and then in only 4 weeks I was able to memorize a deck of cards in less than 2 minutes! Before you knew it I set a record for the fastest to memorize a deck of cards in 1 minute and 27 seconds – on March 7th 2009!!

Learn to trust your memory more, and don't feel like you have to make sure the image is 100% cemented in before you move on to the next item. You will be surprised at how much your memory really does recall.

A great way to work on speed memory is to get a computer program that generates random words, or random numbers. I have programs such as this on my website, www.ronwhitetraining.com. You can calibrate the speed for your purposes, and then speed it up as you get better and better.

The average mind can read 250 words per minute, and with speed-reading, a level of 1000 words per minute or more can be reached. My good friend, Howard Berg, who is in the Guinness Book of World Record as the World's Fastest Reader, says that the #1 thing that slows him down when reading is turning the pages!!

Train for accuracy but also remember to train for speed! Your mind will operate at incredibly fast and efficient levels if you push it!

Things to Do, Directions, Names

Once again it is very simple, to remember anything all you need is:

1. Focus

2. Location

3. Code

4. Action

5. Review

I want you to file your "things to do list" to your skeleton files today. Always start with number one. When I'm ending each day, I will lie in my bed and I'll ask myself, "What do I have to do tomorrow?" I will then file that to my skeleton files. Whenever you go through the process in your day, use your skeleton files. Let's say you have five things to do, and someone calls you during the day and says, "Don't forget to call Tom!" Your picture for Tom is a tomcat. So, you immediately file that to your next open file. That way, throughout the day, you are always adding on. When you complete a task on your files, change the picture somehow.

Set it on fire, or throw water on it. Visualize a big red checkmark, but always use your skeleton files for a "things to do" list for the day. This is a great way to make sure things get done.

Now, how about directions? Have you ever stopped and asked somebody for directions, and then you didn't remember what the guy said? They'll say, "Go down to Maple Street, and take a left, and go two stop signs and take a right. Go to King Street, and take a left and you're there." You drive away thinking, "Great!" And no sooner are you gone you can't recall what they just told you. It happens all the time. This is because right and lefts are abstract. Here is something you can do to recall directions.

Make every right, rain and every left a lamb. So when someone says, "Go down to Maple Street and take a left," file maple syrup and a lamb to your first file. Then they say, "Go two stop signs and make a right." File two stop signs and rain to your next file. Then when they say, "Go to King Street and take a left," file king's crown and a lamb to your number 3 file. What you're doing is simply turning abstracts into pictures. Remember that your mind thinks in pictures, and that is the code your mind needs to recall. What you are filing is pictures for abstracts.

How about this one? You go to a friend's house, and you can't recall where you put your keys. You know, I do this all the time. Every time I set my keys down, where I set them is my file; and the picture, of course, are my keys; and the action is an explosion whenever I set my keys down. My friends don't know it, but when I go to their house I'm exploding all of their furniture. You have a great system in your hands. You can use it to do anything, as long as you put your mind to it. I want to conclude today's program by practicing some numbers and how to turn them into pictures, using phonics. Let's do 10 numbers – 11 through 20. Eleven would be tuh and tuh, so that is tot. Twelve would be tuh and nuh, so that is like a tin can. Number 13 would be tuh and muh, so that is time. Visualize a clock. Number 14 is tuh and ruh, so that would be a tire. Number 15 is tuh and luh, so that would be tile. Sixteen is duh and shuh, so that is dish. Seventeen is tuh and cuh, so that is tack. Eighteen is duh and vuh, so that is dove. Nineteen is tuh and puh, so that is tap. Twenty is nuh and suh, so that is nose.

Phonics is a skill that, if you master, you are going to find yourself with an unstoppable memory. When I get a phone number, I use phonics to file it to my skeleton files. Do I have a day timer for my phone numbers? Absolutely! However, I'm not in a rush to put the numbers in there. When I get a phone number, I use phonics to turn it into a picture, and then I file it away.

Here is a memory test for today. Turn the following names into picture:

Frank	Heidi
Harold	Judy
Tommy	Melissa
George	Missy
Blaine	William
Sally	Davey
Sarah	Barney
Natalie	Jacob
Daniel	Burt
Rebecca	

Memorizing Sub Points

Well, it's Day 27. We're getting closer and closer to making sure you have an instant recall memory. Are you excited? I know I am! You have learned a lot. Feel free to go back and review any portion of this program at any time. There are many sections, like the phonics and names that you need to review. Stick to the basics at first, master them, and then try the advanced stuff.

Today I want to give you some ideas for your files. Your house files can be used for product knowledge and I want to make sure you see that. You have 5 rooms and 5 files in each room. If you were an automobile salesperson, you can dedicate each room to one type of car. If you're a real estate agent, you get listings. Make each room represent an area of town, and then always have 5 listings in each room. That way, when someone says they want a house in a specific area, and you have 5 listings at your mental fingertips about that area, that is a great tool. If you are in any other kind of business, you can file procedures, or sales presentations, or file steps to overcoming objections.

My family is in the furniture refinishing business, marketing to hotels and refinishing their furniture. Occasionally, if I am in a town where they have a hotel they are trying to get work from I will stop by and give a sales presentation. I don't know much about refinishing furniture, but I'll talk to the crew leader back home about what he wants me to say. I will then file that to my skeleton files – whether it is specific steps in restoring the furniture they use in their process, or names of other hotels they have done in the area. I will file the information to my skeleton files and I will sound extremely knowledgeable.

If you're a student, you are going to have to take notes the exact same way you have always done. I hate to break the news to you, but it's true. You still will need to read the chapters the exact same way that you've always done. The difference is, when you study you only have to study once. You know people will always find time to do something over again, but they can never find time to do it right the first time. As a student, that is exactly what you are going to be doing with this system – doing it right the first time.

Let's say you are studying for a history test in your first room. You could make that room the causes of the Civil War. The next room could be the key leaders or battles. Maybe the next room, some of the changes the war brought about. Perhaps you are studying for a psychology test and you make the first room the theories and ideas of Sigmund Freud. The second room could be the theories and ideas of Carl Young. The third room could be five theories or ideas of B. F. Skinner. Perhaps you could simply have a room that lists all the major psychologists. You have a lot of different options with this method, but it all comes down to location, code and action. You must be able to see what you want to recall and see it with a lot of action. That is the key to this whole system.

Now, for our activities, do you remember your city files? Review them quickly. Stop the program if you have to. Mentally file the following 10 items to your city files, remembering to move quickly and use creative items with a lot of action!

1. Sun

2. Mercury

3. Venus

4. Earth

5. Mars

6. Jupiter

7. Saturn

8. Uranus

9. Neptune

10. Pluto

You just memorized the planets in order from the sun! If you wanted you could go back and add an item to each picture. For example, you could turn the miles from the sun into a picture, and place that picture on top of each file as well. Then you would have 2 items on each file and so on. If you want to memorize sub points for something, you do it using the system that we learned with the Mount Rainer story. Remember when you created that story? What if you filed Mount Rainer to your number 1 file? You would actually be filing much more than Mount Rainer to that #1 file you would be filing almost 20 items. If you want to recall sub points to something you will file the initial item or word, and then go back and create layers. File the second "layer," then the third, and fourth and so on. This is how you memorize sub-points!

Alphabet Files

Welcome, my friend! It is Day 28. The most important part of the program is going to be to implement it. You have 25 house files; 10 skeleton files; 20 pencil files; and 10 city files – that is 65 items. There is no doubt in my mind that I could give you 65 words and right now you could get at least 55 of them. That is very impressive guys! What you have is a valuable opportunity. Remember, to get the best benefit from the gym you have to go work out!

Yesterday, I met 4 people. Today as I was driving, I was reviewing their pictures, and the names of their pictures. I met an Andrew with a goatee, and I had ants drawing on a goatee. I met an Elizabeth with glasses, and I had a lizard with bad breath on her glasses. I met a Paul with sideburns. He had a basketball bouncing on his sideburns. Then finally, I met a Tim with bushy eyebrows. He had a tin can on his eyebrows. Did that require a little bit of thought? Yes a little bit. However, is it going to be worth it? You better believe it. Few things are more rewarding than making another person feel special and important, and that is exactly what you do when you recall their name. The same effort you put into names, you will have to consciously put into other areas of this system.

I want to show you another filing system that I have seen used before. Actually, kids really like this one. Not only is it good to use as files, but also when you need to recall letters – such as the letters in product

codes or sequences, this system works on the concept that you must see
something to recall it. It works wonderfully! Here are 26 Alphabet files.

A = Ax

B = Bicycle

C = Computer

D = Drum

E = Ear

F = Fire

G = Grass

H = House

I = Igloo

J = Jet

K = Knight

L = Light

M = Moon

N = Net

O = Octopus

P = Pen

Q = Quilt

R = River

S = Sign

T = Tent

U = Umbrella

V = Vase

W = Wine

X = X Ray

Y = Yo Yo

Z = Zipper

Now, what are these 26 items? Good question. And the answer is – they're whatever you want them to be! If you find yourself in a situation where you see a math formula, and there are letters that keep repeating, these 26 items give you pictures for those letters. They also give you 26 files if you choose to use them for that. This system is meant to give you a system that you can adjust to your own needs. Review it a couple of times if you want, or wherever you encounter a situation where you feel these could be of use, and then come back to them. It could be great for memorizing product codes with letters in them, serial numbers that have letters in them, or license plates. These items all contain letters and now you have pictures for letters!

Keep Your Motivation UP!

Welcome back! Today is Day 29. How did you like your alphabet picture? It was kind of interesting. Today I want to review with you what we have learned. You have learned a system developed by the Romans almost 2,500 years ago to give speeches and presentations without notes. The Romans called this method "Loci," which is the Latin word for places. Guys, what we have done is to establish places in your memory where we are going to store information. Remember they are places that you can see.

The pencil list has 20 files on it. Review them in your mind, and in your guidebook if you have to. The skeleton file has 10 files on it. They are top, nose, mouth, ribs, liver, joint, cap, fibula, ball and sand. Remember that not only are these files, but they also represent the 10 primary phonetic sounds of tuh, nuh, muh, luh, juh, cuh, fuh, puh and suh. Remember, by using phonics we can create new word-pictures that can be used as files to help us recall something.

Our city files and our house files give us 25 plus 10 files for 35 total files. You have 65 files. That should get you through most anything you need to retain. If you are a student, you are still going to have to take your notes just like you always did. You're still going to have to read the chapter and highlight the key information, just like you always did. The difference will come when you go to retain it. You now have a system, and you are going to have to study once and then you'll be done! You will get it right the first time. I find it odd that people can always find something to do over, but they can rarely find time to do it right the first time. This system enables you to do that. When someone gives you their phone number, immediately turn it into a picture and file it to your files. Or, if you want, use their house or office and file a picture to that file – whether it be of their house or their office.

I recently had a student ask me if I could teach them to recall all 213 counties in his state. I said, "Yes!" Now that sounds somewhat overwhelming, but this is what you do when you encounter a situation like that. When you have an overwhelming amount of information to recall, look at it on paper. Most likely you will have to get it on paper anyway. Get it on paper, and then decide how many files you're going to use. If you need more files, add some house or city or even phonics files. Once you have enough files, then break the task down into easy, manageable steps. Set deadlines for each goal. Once you do that, you will not be attempting a huge memory feat, you will be attempting several small feats, and that is what this course is full of. You should be very well equipped right now to handle just about every situation that you encounter.

I would like to tell you the story of a west Texas millionaire rancher. He had a party for his daughter to attract all the suitable bachelors around. This is what we call in sales as "group prospecting." The night was full of food, and music, and dancing. After everyone had fun, the west Texas rancher asked everyone to gather around an Olympic-size swimming pool located out back. He had the foresight to stock this pool with alligators and water moccasins – not very pleasant. He stood at the end of the pool and he said, "I will make an offer to the first man to dive into this pool and swim the length of it." He said. "I will offer him the choice of 3 things: Number one, he can have one million dollars in cold, hard cash; number two, he can have 5,000 acres of my best land; and number 3, you could have my beautiful daughter in marriage. Gentlemen, obviously, if you take the hand of my daughter, one day all of this will be yours because one day this will all be hers." Well, no sooner had the words left his mouth, and there was a splash at one end of the pool. A young man emerged at the other end, and he had just set a world's record that will never be eclipsed. The rancher was so excited, he ran over and said, "Son, I guess you want something!" The young man said, "Yes, sir." The rancher said, "Well, tell me, son, what is it that you want? Do you want the million dollars in cold, hard cash?" The young man said, "No, sir." He said, "Well, son, do you want the 5,000 acres of my best land?" And the young man said, "No, sir." The west Texas rancher said, "Well then, son, I'm assuming that you want the hand of my beautiful daughter in marriage." The young man said, "No, sir." The rancher was shocked! He said, "Son, if you don't want the hand of my beautiful daughter in marriage, you don't want the cash, you don't want the land, son, tell me what it is you want." The young man said, "I want to know the name of that dude who pushed me into the end of the swimming pool."

Now, I think you'll agree that this man was highly motivated. Once he hit the water, he had a goal to get out, and he did. In life you are going to be thrown out there for the water moccasins and the alligators, but I want to encourage you to keep your eyes on the goal. This system is worth more than any reward you can imagine. It will increase your self-esteem; it will increase your confidence; it will increase your knowledge; and increase your ability to build relationships by recalling a person's name.

Stay motivated to practice this system, even if you have to imagine alligators chasing you!

My challenge to you is to create more mental journeys, like the ones we did with your city and your house. Select different areas of town, and memorize 20-30 files on each journey. Perhaps you select 5 areas of town and 30 files on each journey, which will give you 150 files right there!

After this, select 5-10 of your family members' homes, friends' homes, or favorite hangout spots, and build 20-30 files in each of these. Upon completion of these activities you could literally have 300-500 files in a week or so! At the publishing of this book I have around 2900 files!

Review and a New Beginning

Welcome to the final day! It's Day 30! How are you today? My friend, I have enjoyed this journey. I hope that you have as well. This has been a journey that is not coming to an end; you are now simply taking a fork in the road. Actually, this is the beginning of the road. Now is the time that you take what you have learned and apply it to your life. You are like a bird flying out of the nest. Right now you should have some motivation to apply this system. If that motivation ever wanes, I encourage you to come back to this course and remind yourself of why you got so excited in the first place. Motivation is an important part of any learning process, and I encourage you not to let the learning process end here, and I am not specifically talking about memory training. There are some very interesting books and recorded programs on memory training; in addition there is a tremendous amount of knowledge out there at your fingertips.

You could listen to Napoleon Hill's book, *Think and Grow Rich*, or Og Mandino's *The Greatest Salesman In The World*, or my fellow Texan Zig Ziglar's book, *See You At The Top*. Do you know what the exciting thing is? It is the ability to file knowledge shared with you in these trainings to your files, and retain the information for as long as you like! That is exciting!

A University of California study reveals that a person living in Los Angeles could acquire the equivalent of a two-year college degree in three years of normal driving time by listening to recorded programs. The total amount of time that you invest if you do it while driving would almost be zero! Imagine that! I have never seen a disc jockey jump out of a radio and cut you a check for listening while you are driving, however, every time you listen to a training or an educational program, you get better and better. Now the people who listen to the correct recorded programs are the happiest, most well adjusted, excited people I know. Now combine that with a solid reading program and you are really in business! The rule is this, while you are riding – listen, and while you are sitting – read.

I recently heard a man I respect very much say that many men desire peace, yet few men desire the things that lead to peace. We all want the prize at the end of the tunnel, yet few men desire the things that lead to the prize. To get the prize in your life you must pay the price. The people who listen to the motivational programs, or read positive educational books, are often the ones who need it the least. They're already successful. When I go to the gym, the people I see there are in such great shape I wonder why they're in the gym! The ones that are successful in life didn't all of a sudden adopt their reading habits when they were already successful. They are there because of their habits. Good habits are difficult to acquire, but very easy to live with. I encourage you to develop good habits in this educational arena. Constantly challenge your memory with knowledge.

You have a tremendous skill. Very few people have the ability to meet a roomful of people and recall their names, or give a 7 hour talk and never access a note, or memorize a chapter of a book, or obtain a list of 65 items after hearing them once. Guys, you have that ability. It is in this system. Whether you know it or not, you have just placed yourself in a very select group. I encourage you to take advantage of this tremendous opportunity. I look forward to meeting you one day and hearing your personal success stories. I enjoyed our journey together and I hope that you did as well.

I will leave you with this thought. It is not what you eat, but what you digest that makes you healthy. It is not what you earn, but what you invest that makes you wealthy. And it is not what you learn, but what you remember that makes you wise. John F. Kennedy paraphrased a verse out of Luke in the New Testament that said, "To those who much is given, much is expected." My friends, you have been given much, now much is expected.

Get Your Bonus Video of
USA Memory Champion Ron White
teaching you:

- How to Give Speeches Without Notes

- How to Memorize Poems, Quotes and Scriptures

- How to Memorize Math and Chemistry Formulas

- How to Easily Memorize Six and Seven-Digit Numbers

- How to Memorize a Deck of Playing Cards

http://www.increase-your-memory.com

AUTHOR'S BIOGRAPHY

Ron White is without question the nation's number one memory expert, and one of the leading experts in the world.

His professional vitae includes:

- Two-Time USA <u>Memory Champion</u> (2009 and 2010).

- Held record for fastest person to memorize a deck of cards in the USA (1.27 minutes) for two years.

- Appeared on Stan Lee's Super Humans on the History Channel.

- An eight-year Veteran of the US Navy (served tour in Afghanistan in 2007).

- He has spoken globally on memory skills in countries such as Puerto Rico, Canada, the Bahamas, Singapore, Malaysia, Bangkok, Spain, Belgium, Australia and even Nebraska, USA.

- Ron has been speaking on memory to business professionals and students since 1991. His talks include, "Triple Your Memory and Triple Your Business." And "Memory Power = Student Power."

- He has appeared on FOX and "Friends"; Good Morning America, the CBS Early Show; ABC World News Tonight; the Martha Stewart Show; CBS Evening News; the Discovery Channel; and hundreds of national and international radio and print media venues.

Get a FREE video of Ron teaching advanced memory techniques at:

http://www.increase-your-memory.com

Other Books from Laurenzana Press

The Strangest Secret by Earl Nightingale

How To Write a Book This Weekend, Even If You Flunked English Like I Did by Vic Johnson

52 Mondays: The One Year Path To Outrageous Success and Lifelong Happiness by Vic Johnson

Persistence & Perseverance: Dance Until It Rains by The Champions Club

The Law of Attraction: How To Get What You Want by Robert Collier

Time Management Tips: 101 Best Ways to Manage Your Time by Lucas McCain

Get Motivated: 101 Best Ways to Get Started, Keep Going and Finish Strong by Lucas McCain

Successful & Healthy Aging: 101 Best Ways to Feel Younger & Live Longer by Lisa J. Johnson

Self Confidence Secrets: How To Be Outgoing and Overcome Shyness by Lucas McCain

Happiness Habits: 21 Secrets to Living a Fun and Outrageously Rewarding Life by Lucas McCain

Self Help Books: The 101 Best Personal Development Classics by Vic Johnson

Overcoming Fear: 101 Best Ways to Overcome Fear and Anxiety and Take Control of Your Life Today! by Lucas McCain

Public Speaking Fear? 21 Secrets To Succeed In Front of Any Crowd by Lucas McCain

Going Green: 101 Ways To Save A Buck While You Save The Earth by Lucas McCain

Stress Management: 101 Best Ways to Relieve Stress and Really Live Life by Lucas McCain

Other Books from Laurenzana Press

Should I Divorce? 11 Questions To Answer Before You Decide to Stay or Go by Jennifer Jessica

Divorce Recovery: 101 Best Ways To Cope, Heal And Create A Fabulous Life After a Divorce by Lisa J. Johnson

Should I Have a Baby? 10 Questions to Answer BEFORE You Get Pregnant by Jennifer Jessica

Stop Procrastinating: 101 Best Ways to Overcome Procrastination NOW! by Lucas McCain

Think and Grow Rich: The Lost Secret by Vic Johnson

Should I Get Married? 10 Questions to Answer Before You Say I Do by Jennifer Jessica

Meditation Techniques: How To Meditate For Beginners And Beyond by Lucas McCain

Fast NLP Training: Persuasion Techniques To Easily Get What You Want by Lucas McCain

How To Attract a Woman: The Secret Handbook of What Women Want in a Man by Jennifer Jessica

Cure Anxiety Now! 21 Ways To Instantly Relieve Anxiety & Stop Panic Attacks by Lucas McCain

Should I Get Married? 10 Questions to Answer Before You Say I Do by Jennifer Jessica

CPSIA information can be obtained at www.ICGtesting.com
Printed in the USA
LVOW01s2025110614

389613LV00030B/1609/P